A Passion for Africa

Books by Stanley Wally Hoffman
(listed in chronological order)

To a Land He Showed Us
In the Tanganyika Bush
Tracks in the Dust
Amid Perils Often
Long Shadows
A Passion for Africa

A Passion for Africa

Stanley Wally Hoffman

VANTAGE PRESS
New York

To my grandchildren:

Ashling, Natasha, Jesse, Courtney, Shaina,
Mikaela, Logan, Sean, and Erik

who were either born in Africa,
or are being raised in Africa.

(Tiffany, my first grandchild, had a book
dedicated to her earlier.)

"I am with you and will watch over you wherever you go, and I will bring you back to this land. I will not leave you until I have done what I have promised you."

—Genesis 28:15

"The Lord stood at my side and gave me strength, so that through me the message might be fully proclaimed and all the Gentiles might hear it."

—2 Timothy 4:17

"I have fought the good fight, I have finished the race, I have kept the faith."

—2 Timothy 4:7

Contents

Preface

This is my final book in a series of books I have written on experiences I have had while serving the Lord in the various countries of Africa. In this book, *A Passion for Africa,* I will take you into five countries in Southern Africa and again share accounts in the present tense as I have done in all of my previous books.

In *A Passion for Africa,* I will continue my story from where I left off in my previous book *Long Shadows.* It concludes my life as a missionary for thirty-seven years on the continent of Africa.

I have taken time to share what God has done with my life throughout the years in Africa in order that those who follow after me will know what took place; how and when it occurred. Much has happened! Time to share it in churches I have travelled to, and with individuals I have talked to, was never long enough to do the Lord justice for the way He blessed and kept me.

So here now is the concluding book that I have compiled of my years on the mission field.

Introduction

Today as I sit with my diaries in front of me and commence to write the final book of my years in Southern Africa, I find myself in a melancholy mood. An era in my life has come to an end! My years of tramping up and down the African soil with the gospel of Christ have finally run out. For some people living thirty-seven years in Third World countries may seem never ending, but for me they went by all too quickly. They have been wonderful years never to be forgotten. It has been a very fulfilling and thrilling life!

Not only has the Lord granted me health and strength throughout all the years but also safety. Countless miles have been covered without a major mishap. Surely, He has spared me for His service. It has not been easy, but at the same time it has not been too difficult either. He knew of what I was capable. Years on end, I have had to be the one to preach and to teach others—seldom being the recipient of the Word. Marion has reminded me often that I have not lost any of my oomph; in fact, she says that I kept accomplishing more as the years progressed than in those earlier years. If this is true, then I have only the Lord to thank for the strength He continued to give me.

My leaving Africa after years of walking its paths and traveling its roads is a painful one. No one is forcing me to leave, and yet I am leaving. I do not really want to leave, and yet I am leaving. The African church leaders have pointed out to me that nowhere in the Scriptures does it say that a servant of the Lord is to retire at the age of seventy years. In fact, they add that many were called at eighty into the service of the Lord, such as Moses and Abraham! Then what is it? It is something beyond my control. The mission's manual states that missionaries are to retire at sixty-five, no later than seventy, and return to their homeland. So there it is!

All the fanfare that goes with retirement from the field has taken place and various gifts were lovingly bestowed upon us as we visited our supporting churches for the last time. Global Missions honored us with a plaque expressing their deepest gratitude for our thirty-seven years of missionary service in Africa. Recognition also came from the Western Canadian Church of God for services rendered overseas. Then Warner Pacific College bestowed upon Marion and myself Honorary Doctorates of Humane Letters on May 4, 2002, in recognition of our nearly four decades of missionary service on behalf of the Church of God.

Finally, Gardner College (previously Alberta Bible Institute) awarded both of us with Doctor of Divinity degrees on April 27, 2003. That same day I was also elected to membership on the honor society of Association of Canadian Bible Colleges. After years of giving myself fully to the ministry of our Lord in Africa, I have been well received by my countrymen since returning from the mission field.

There were times when alone out in the heart of Africa on my safaris into the interior, I would often gaze up at the night sky and wonder how many back in America there were that really were thinking of me at that very moment? They certainly did not know where I was just then! Did they even care? Quite often even Marion did not know in which faraway village I would be bedded down for the night. How long would it take for them to find me? I ended up consoling myself that it was the Lord whom I was serving and that He does know where I am and that He cares!

Since then I have discovered that many did remember me and are now showing their gratitude for services rendered in Africa. My passion for Africa did not go entirely unnoticed. It was a great life while it lasted. It could not have been better! My days as a career missionary are over, to my lasting regret. But I can still look back over that long stretch of years and recall those precious moments with the Lord. The miles I walked with the Master, and then the miles He carried me because the road got too rocky. It is not possible to turn back the clock but, oh, how I would love to live those years once more!

This, my final book, will therefore end an era of missionary work in my beloved Africa that has given me so much to remember. Live over again with me some of the most fulfilling days of my life as a missionary. Experience with me the feelings that I myself felt during those safaris to remote villages in the interior of Southern Africa.

Southern Africa

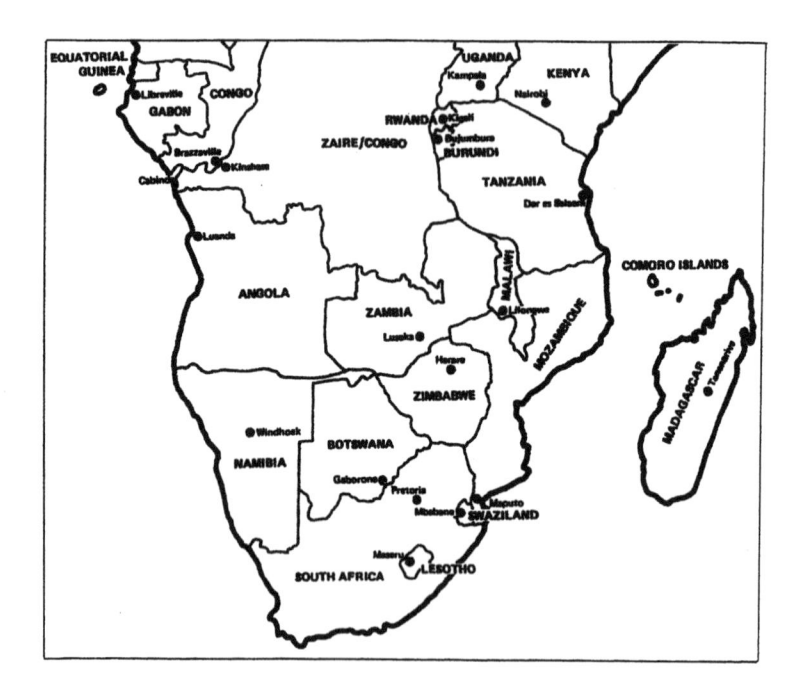

A Passion for Africa

One
Southern Africa

Africa, with its 56 countries, is the second largest continent, covering 30,244,000 square kilometers of the earth's surface with a population of approximately 800 million people. Sahara, the world's largest desert, and the River Nile, the world's longest river (6,695 kilometers), are both located in Africa. At Murchison Falls in Uganda, the mighty Nile squeezes through a narrow 5.5 meter gap! The highest point on the continent is snowcapped Mt. Kilimanjaro (5,895 meters) in Tanzania. The longest lake in the world is Lake Tanganyika (677 kilometers) and it is also the second deepest (1,433 meters) in the world. The largest falls in the world is Victoria Falls (1.6 kilometres wide and 110 meters deep) and located on the Zambezi River at the Zambia–Zimbabwe border. Lake Victoria in East Africa is the second largest freshwater lake in the world.

Marion and I have had the privilege of sharing the gospel in ten different countries in Africa; in nine of those we were pioneers. In this book I am sharing experiences that we have had with the Lord in five of the countries in Southern Africa. They are: Zimbabwe, Mozambique, Malawi, Angola, and also continue with those we had in Zambia. My sphere of work continued to increase annually! The Lord gave me the privilege of seeing souls saved in these Southern African countries. For this I praise Him!

Zambia lies just south of Tanzania and the Congo, and then north of Zimbabwe. Malawi is its neighbor to the east and Angola to the west. Other countries that share borders with Zambia are Mozambique, Botswana, and Namibia. The main attraction is the magnificent Victoria Falls on the Zambezi River. The Zambezi River is the fourth longest in Africa after the Nile, Congo, and Niger. It begins its journey from under a tree in northwestern Zambia and flows south and then east for 2,700 kilometers before finally reaching the Indian Ocean. It also has fascinating parks such as the Luangwa and the Kafue where animals and birds abound in plenty.

The area of Zambia is 752,615 square kilometers and it had a population of 7.4 million when we moved there in 1989, but has since grown to 10.6 million in 2001. Before gaining its independence from Great Britain in 1964, it was called Northern Rhodesia. Zambia gets its name from the Zambezi River. Lusaka is its capital and English is still its official language. Livingstone was the first capital, from 1905 until 1935. Its currency is the Zambia Kwacha. Bemba appears to be the largest ethnic group with Nyanja and Tonga second and third. Christianity (Protestants) makes up 34 percent of the population and the Roman Catholics 26 percent with the Muslims only 2 percent. The remainder still adhere to their traditional and tribal beliefs.

Many of the tribal customs that exist in Zambia are injurious to its people. One of those practiced widely is known as the cleansing custom. When a husband or wife dies, it is compulsory that the survivor be cleansed by having sex with an in-law. This is one of the reasons that the nation today is gripped with an epidemic of AIDS (Acquired Immune Deficiency Syndrome). Both sexes are affected equally with this disease. Orphans are plentiful, as we also discovered while in Uganda. We are trusting that the gospel we have brought to this nation will stem the tide and turn many away to live a holy life.

Zimbabwe is a landlocked country in southern Africa. It is surrounded by: Zambia to the north, Mozambique to the east, South Africa to the south, and Botswana to the west. It has an area of 390,580 square kilometers with a population of nearly 11 million people. It gained its independence in 1980, changing its name from Rhodesia to Zimbabwe. Zimbabwe is a Shona word, meaning "house of stone." Harare, once known as Salisbury, is the capital city. The Zimbabwe dollar is their currency.

The ethnic background is Bantu, with Shona being the dominant people (71 percent), and with Ndebele a distant second (16 percent). The official language remains English. Traditional tribal beliefs are still popular (40 percent). What about Christianity? Statistics differ, but a figure I have come across suggests it to be 24 percent. The figure is higher if you include those who have combined their traditional beliefs with Christianity (35 percent). The Muslims have only 1 percent. It is to this country we have taken the gospel of Christ.

In early 2000, the government of President Mugabe stepped up its policy to retrieve land from the white farmers in order to resettle them with the country's have-nots. Determined to retain power at all costs, he declared it was now taking back what had been stolen from their ancestors. Mobs of young men claiming to be veterans of the 1980 War for Independence began arriving at farms and claiming everything on them to now be their property, The so-called "war veterans" forcibly moved many farmers off their land, brutally murdering or maiming some of them in the process—including the black Zimbabwean laborers. As a result, it is bringing chaos to this country's economy and the situation is continuing to steadily deteriorate. Corruption is running wild in a country that faces both starvation and financial ruin. Sadly, at the writing of this book, there is still no end in sight to this senseless rape of the land.

Mozambique borders the Indian Ocean in southeastern Africa. It was recognized as a Portuguese colony in 1885 and became known as Portuguese East Africa. In 1964 a guerrilla war opposing Portuguese rule was launched and lasted ten years. After a year with an interim government, Mozambique gained its independence in 1975. That same year the opposition group led an armed struggle against the government that lasted seventeen years. The civil war, combined with severe droughts, caused so much human suffering that Mozambique was declared Africa's poorest country from 1975 to 1992. Today it is still one of Africa's poorest nations, being rebuilt from scratch.

The area of Mozambique is 801,590 square kilometers and has a population of 17 million people. The capital city is Maputo, once called Lourenzo Marques during the colonial days. Their currency is the Metical (plural, Meticais). The official language is still Portuguese but in the villages there are Bantu dialects such as Makua, Tonga, Nyanja, Sena, and Shona. All of the many African groups of Mozambique are of Bantu ancestry. Religious beliefs are very diverse with strong animistic practices. Therefore, traditional tribal beliefs are very much in the majority (58 percent), Christianity (mainly Roman Catholic) is second (31 percent), and, finally, Islam (11 percent). A field that is white onto harvest!

Malawi is a landlocked country in southern Africa and lies on the floor of the Great Rift Valley, which extends from the Red Sea to Mozambique. In the early nineteenth century, this area was a center of slave trade when Arabs with dhows carried their human cargo to the Far East. Missionaries helped to stamp it out, Livingstone being one of them. In 1891, Britain made this area a British protectorate. Nyasaland, as it was previously known, gained its independence in 1964 and became the nation of Malawi. Today, it ranks among the world's least developed countries.

The area of Malawi is 118,480 square kilometers with a population of nearly 10 million people. Lilongwe is the capitol and their currency is the Malawi Kwacha. The official languages are English and Chewa (Nyanja). All of their tribal groups are of Bantu heritage. They are: Chewa, Tonga, Tumbuka, Lomwe, Yao, and Ngoni. Half of the people call themselves Christians (50 percent), but traditional beliefs still persist (30 percent), with Muslims on the rise (20 percent). We want to assist with the spreading of the gospel in this country where Dr. David Livingstone preached it a century ago. What a challenge!

Angola is a large country in southwestern Africa on the Atlantic coast. The Portuguese established themselves on the coast of Angola near the close of the fifteenth century, but did not obtain complete control over the interior until the end of the nineteenth century. It became important as a source of slaves for Brazil, Portugal's large colony in South America. After the decline of the slave trade, Portuguese settlers began to develop the land. Portugal finally agreed to grant independence to Angola in 1975.

A civil war immediately broke out between the ruling MPLA (Popular Movement for the Liberation of Angola) party that formed the government and UNITA (National Union for the Total Independence of Angola), the opposing party. It became the longest running civil war in Africa, which just came to a shaky end when Jonas Savimbi, the leader of UNITA, was killed in early 2002. The economy has been crippled with one and a half million lives lost in fighting! It has been called the worst war in the world. Many more will die of starvation due to the devastation brought on by the guerrilla war. Relief agencies are slowly trickling in to help. Restrictions still apply for foreigners wishing to travel outside the city limits of Luanda.

It has an area of 1,246,700 square kilometers with a population of 11 million people where 72 percent of them make a meagre living by farming. The capital city is Luanda and the official language is Portuguese. Their currency is the Kwanza. Three of the larger ethnic groups are the Ovimbundu at 37 percent, Mbundu at 22 percent, and Kongo at 13 percent. Religiously, 38 percent of them are Roman Catholic, 13 percent are Protestants, and 47 percent have indigenous beliefs. A vast field of souls is waiting to be harvested for the Lord! Due to the long civil war, it was not possible for anyone to visit Angola except on government-approved business. Thus spiritual darkness still covers much of the land. How I have longed to walk among them and share Christ with them. It is a passion that does not want to leave me!

*   *   *

I suppose demon-possession and witchcraft, two of the most powerful forces of darkness still existing in Southern Africa, will continue to do well so long as Christians remain at ease in Zion. Spirit possession is still a common occurrence with most tribes. For instance, many men and women and even some children of the Korekore tribe in the Zambezi Valley gather periodically to dance out their possessing spirits! They believe famine and drought are due to the anger of the spirits and therefore must be contacted and appeased through their hosts or mediums. These spirits control the rainfall and the fertility of the land. Shop holders, traders, and even bus owners make gifts to spirit mediums in order to ensure that their business prospers.

With the Korekore and Shona people of Zimbabwe, lions and humans are the hosts most commonly chosen by male guardians, while female spirit guardians favor the python. After a period of dwelling in the host and wandering in the forest, the spirit becomes restless and desires to speak through a human host. The spirit then leaves the lion and seeks out a man. The man, after the spirit enters him behaves as though he were mad, eats raw meat like an animal, and wanders about in the forest! We have personally dealt with these kind of possessed people.

Witchcraft is still practiced today among the Shona people. It is not uncommon to find a witch in most all the villages. While men use "black" medicine that brings about physical harm, it is the women that control nearly all other forms of witchcraft. The witch called an *nganga* travels by night, usually riding on the back of a hyena to get to where it is going. The Wambugwe that we worked with in Tanzania believed as well that their witches, in order to carry out their evil deeds, rode around at night on hyenas. (*To a Land He Showed Us*, chapter six.)

Although the Shona believe in God, they also believe in their ancestral spirits called *vadzimu* (plural). When a person dies his spirit wanders around until it is given permission to come back and dwell in their midst. If a person, usually a relative, welcomes the ancestral spirit *mudzimu* to possess him or her then it does so. This person now has become the medium or host and is given special abilities. It is impossible to rid oneself of his or her own *mudzimu*, unless a man of God casts it out. We have been able to do this frequently during our travels in Africa.

Many tribes, such as the Chewa tribe of Malawi and the Sena of Mozambique, believe all deaths and most illnesses are attributed to sorcery. Natural death is possible but only when a man or woman has reached the end of his or her given period here on earth. But rarely does this happen with the Chewa people. And so it is that they leave sick people till they are beyond hope of recovery before they bring them for medical attention. This has been a common occurrence throughout our years in the African bush. With witchcraft so widespread, it is most difficult for the newly converted Christian to shed that life of living in fear. He or she has been taught that life is tied to taboos from one's birth until death.

Before closing this chapter, I want to point out that the Luvale and Lunda tribes in northwestern Zambia and the Luchazi, Chokwe, and Mbunda tribes across the border in Angola share many traditional ceremonies that are not found elsewhere in Southern Africa. They are fond of wearing masks and costumes that are quite exaggerated to say the least. There are a few other tribes, such as the Ngoni and Nyao, that too wear masks during their dances and ceremonies but they are not believed to be spirits that have risen from the grave, as do the aforementioned tribes! These spirits are called *makishi*.

The dancer inside the costume is usually a possessed person, one who is able to associate with ancestral spirits. The heavily decorated performer is therefore a rare creature returned from the dead. It takes on all shapes and sizes, some walk on two poles, others resemble birds, animals, or various hideous creatures. Drums are used during these ceremonies. Their dances, which are varied, can last for two days and nights. Some of them are quite sensual where eventually men and women pair off for the night. The Luvale dancers are well noted for their suggestive movements. Of course, most dances in Africa fall into this category.

Opportunities to share the gospel in these countries of Southern Africa are endless. That is if you do not mind leaving the well-beaten tracks for the footpaths that lead you into villages scattered in the bush or among the rocks. And then to sit with them on their short wooden stools in front of their grass-roofed huts and listen to their stories of customs and traditions that have been handed down to them through the ages, taboos that still play such an important role in their everyday life and interfere with their walk for God! Finally, you share of what the Lord is able to do for them. How the Savior can lead them out of a life of fear for the unknown into one of trusting God for their every need. Oh what opportunities await the soul seekers!

The bush missionary is a dying breed. Their ranks are thinning out and memories of them are dimming. Books about them can only be found on shelves of old bookshops. Yet, some dare to live on! They keep giving of themselves so long as God will direct them. I treasure the memories of those years that I have spent in Eastern, Central, and Southern Africa. Much knowledge was gained from the villagers as I sat and listened to their tales of hardship and woe. More than once have I, in thought, found myself again in their company of former times. It is most satisfying to look back to those happy days in the bush!

Come with me now into the countries of Southern Africa as I share the gospel in the villages of Zimbabwe, Mozambique, Malawi, Angola, and Zambia.

Zimbabwe

Two
Crossing into Zimbabwe

When Marion and I moved from Uganda to Zambia in 1989, I began praying for the door to open into neighboring Zimbabwe. We already have several churches along the Zambezi River on the Zambia side, so what is keeping us back from crossing over with the gospel? The answer is that we have no contact person across the border. Then one day one of our pastors in Lusaka, Afunika Tembo, shares with me that he had spent a short time in Zimbabwe awhile back. Great! We begin planning a trip in order to spy out the land for a future ministry in this country to our south.

It is March 4th 1992, when we start out on our safari to Harare. For a week now I have been nursing a sore throat and am still not back to normal. Each night I have been perspiring profusely, going through more towels and nightshirts than any previous time when with a fever. Though weak, I am not going to postpone this trip. The devil has been attacking us for the last couple of days, and Marion and I have had to take a firm stand against him. It takes effort from both of us to avoid him defeating us.

We cross the border without any kind of a delay at either Immigration or Customs on both sides. Marion has prepared a lunch and we eat it as we travel along. An odd noise comes from under the Nissan Patrol and I stop to investigate it. I fail to find the root of the problem. After stopping two more times when the noise reoccurs, Marion prays over it and we continue on our way. There is no further incidence! Praise the Lord! We reach Harare before dark. After supper we retire for the night. It is still early, but I am exhausted. Marion puts her hands on me and prays for my recovery before we turn out the lights.

Tembo and Afeck Lungu, one of our national leaders in Zambia, had gone on ahead of us several days ago in order to meet a distant relative of Tembo and find out the feasibility of planting a church in Harare. We meet them at the prearranged spot in the city and they have a Zimbabwean with them. His name is Eddison and, yes, he would like to work with us. We visit with him at length and discover there are two prospective places in the city and one at Muriel Mines north of Harare, where there are acquaintances of his who may be interested in meeting us. A service is arranged for Sunday morning at a house in Highfield, a suburb of Harare.

The following day we are kept quite busy downtown getting the *Constitution and Bylaws* for Zimbabwe typed out so that they are ready for the upcoming new church here in Zimbabwe. Marion and I also do some shopping. There are more things available in the shops here than in Lusaka.

The service finally gets underway at ten o'clock. There are eighteen of us present. Many that they thought would show up do not. Marion and I sing a duet, after which I preach the message. Eight come forward for salvation and three are anointed for healing. We also pray for one who is oppressed by demons. After the service, we have them choose deacons to lead this new congregation. Pray for them before making our departure. We have planted our first church in Zimbabwe! Thank you, Lord!

On our trip back to Zambia, we drop Eddison at the turn-off to Muriel Mines, near the town of Banket. Lungu and Tembo had stopped in there on their way to Harare and Eddison is now to do a follow-up. We pray for him before we leave him. There are good prospects for a new congregation, Tembo informs us. We will stop in there on our next trip to Zimbabwe.

This we do two months later. We are taking Lungu along to assist us in explaining the organizational structure of our church. It takes us an hour to get through the border this time. The Zimbabwean side was crowded with passengers traveling on several buses. We stop at Cloud's End for some soft drinks to go along with the sandwiches that Marion has brought along. Before reaching Harare we turn off the tarmac road and drive to Muriel Mines, situated 35 kilometers east among some hills. We are disappointed that Eddison, whom we had dropped off on our last trip to check about starting a church here, failed to do so. Before we leave, we appoint one of those that Lungu had met on his previous visit to come to Harare for the service on Sunday.

There are twenty-two of us present at the Sunday service. Several come over from Mufakose, our second prospective congregation, as they did the last time we were here. Lungu shows up with Eddison and his wife. Seven accept Christ after my message and three who are sick request prayer for healing. Three oppressed by evil spirits are dealt with as well. New deacons are appointed as the previous ones have failed to perform their duties. After the meal that was prepared by the women of the house, three men write their tests in Book One of the TEE (Theological Education by Extension) program. They make a passing mark but just. Finally, Lungu teaches for an hour before we take leave and return to our motel.

I felt malaria coming on earlier today and tonight I break down with chills followed by a high fever. It is a tough night. I must have been delirious at one time as I am with two others who are in the same condition as myself. They appear to be Africans. In my delirium, I do not know whether I am suffering from malaria or strep throat. The fever finally breaks in the morning. After a hot bath I feel better except for pain behind my eyes and aches along my back. They slowly subside as the day wears on. We hear on the radio that Lawrence Welk has died of pneumonia at the age of eighty-seven. He is a distant relative of mine on my mother's side.

As we are returning to Zambia, the front tire on the driver's side suddenly goes flat. With the Lord's help, I am able to keep the vehicle on the road. Replace it with the spare and we carry on. It does not take long at the border and we are back in Zambia again. Before driving on to Lusaka, we turn off east at Chirundu and, as last time, hold a service with our church in Pembere, a village near the Zambezi River. I preach the message and many come forward seeking salvation. Also pray for the thirty-two children who are being dedicated to the Lord. There is a shortage of food in this area. People are beginning to eat wild fruit in order to survive. We take along three men with us to Chirundu and buy for them bags of mealie meal at the shop to take back to the village. Mealie meal is maize ground up into flour, a staple food in most of black Africa. We reach home before dark.

On our following trip to Zimbabwe, we discover that Eddison has not been doing anything to strengthen the two congregations in Harare, nor at Muriel Mines, so he is promptly dismissed as our contact person in Zimbabwe. We will pray and wait on the Lord for someone new to come along.

While outside a shopping center we are approached by two white men who beg us for a loaf of bread to eat. They are both poorly dressed and have not eaten for days. One is an old man, while the other one is younger and wearing an earring. My first impulse was to turn my back and walk away. How can there be white men begging in downtown Harare? They explain that there are no jobs available and they have nothing to their name. If we do not assist them, they will starve. Marion and I enter one of the shops and purchase groceries enough to last them a couple of days. They thank us over and over for the gift of food we give them.

After the Sunday morning service where six come forward for prayer, we decide to drive out to Mango Village 150 kilometers east of Harare in Murehwa District so as to meet a relative of one of our members in the Mufakose congregation. We wish to find out whether there is a possibility of planting a church in that village. The chief is glad to see us and grants us permission to start a church in his area. We give him the customary gift plus a Bible. I share with the people who gather and they beg us to return soon. We promise that we will.

It is time to start our journey back to Zambia. We return to the shopping center for a few last items and to fill up the Nissan with fuel. We do not see the two white men who had begged us for food two days earlier. They had told us that they hung out here daily. When we ask whether anyone knew about them, we are given a blank stare. "What white men?" they reply. Who then were they? Were they angels in disguise sent to try us, whether we would respond to white beggars as well as we normally do to the African needy? That was close, but we passed the compassionate test!

On our next safari to plant more churches in Zimbabwe, we also have an opportunity to assist the needy in the Zambezi Valley on the Zimbabwean side of the river. There is a famine out here due to the drought. We purchase fifty bags of mealie meal in Harare and transport them over 300 kilometers north to Kabvuma, a remote village in Guruve District. We run out of tarmac long before we reach our destination. It is especially rough as we commence dropping down into the valley. We spot elephants along the escarpment road.

Our first service takes place at Gubwa Village where twenty-four people have gathered to hear the Word of God. Four accept Christ after my message. Bags of mealie meal are passed out to the needy families before we drive on to our second service that is at Kabvuma Village. Here over 100 people have come out to hear us. I preach and at least thirty-five kneel and receive Christ into their hearts. A committee is chosen plus the church leader, who is Stafford Madzula. We pray for them and close the meeting. Marion hands out the remaining bags of mealie meal. After saying farewell to our newly planted church, we head back to Harare. It's been a long day, but a successful one!

Marion wakes up with a sore back and leg from the strenuous trip yesterday. She will remain behind at the motel while I travel to Mango Village in Murehwa District. Lungu and two other men are riding with me. Two hours later we arrive and find one of the young men we had met on our previous visit locked up in jail. He had raped his cousin and will now spend two years in prison. This has caused quite a disturbance in the village. I leave the men that came with me to do some visitation work while I return to Harare. There is hunger in this hot and dry district and I make plans to return tomorrow with mealie meal for the needy families. Everywhere huge boulders strew the landscape reflecting even more the sun's rays onto this already parched land.

I again leave Marion at the motel. She is much better but needs to stay off the rough roads for another day. I had given her a back massage last night and that has helped some to relieve the pain. The village of Mango appears to be a very dark place! Most of those who gather for the service are young people. After the message nearly all of them seek salvation. A leader and his committee are then chosen. We pray for them. I believe a church has really been planted this time!

In the afternoon we start another church in Kugombo Village. Here we find seventy-three present to hear the Word of God. Several come forward for salvation and others for healing. The new leader they have chosen is Bero. I give out fifteen bags of mealie meal to families needing help. Five bags were passed out earlier in Mango Village. I return to Harare worn out. Marion fared well while I was away. We will be returning to Lusaka in the morning.

*　　*　　*

I am loaded down with Bibles and tracts as I pull out the yard, after having prayer with Marion and the workers. I also am taking along my sleeping bag so that I can sleep in the vehicle should the need arise as I plan to be gone a week. Marion wants to work on the used clothing in the container and is therefore not accompanying me this time, but Lungu is along. Soon after we cross into Zimbabwe, an elephant lumbers across the road in front of us. I pull in at our favorite spot called Cloud's End, near Makuti, for a bite to eat and a soft drink. When we reach Harare, I drop Lungu off at Mufakose so he can visit with his friends and I book in at the motel.

In the morning I meet Lungu who has someone with him who is interested in our church. He is Dzingai Guni who has had some training at an interdenominational Bible School. We have a lengthy discussion and it may be that this new man will become one of our national leaders. Marion and I have been praying earnestly for someone to come along to assist us in establishing a church in this country. I take him along to see about registering the Church of God in Zimbabwe with the EFZ (Evangelical Fellowship of Zimbabwe). This is the only form of recognition that Zimbabwe has for evangelical churches to operate within the country. When our visit with EFZ is done, we separate and call it a day.

Check out early and after picking up Lungu and Guni, I drive out to Mango Village. No one is expecting us. So we check at Kugombo Village and here it is the same. We still do not have a proper leader here in Murehwa District. We are then led to Matsenga Village about 10 kilometers distance where they want us to start a church. Again, no one is prepared. We find only a woman pounding maize. We pray with her and leave. There are some rock paintings nearby so we walk out to inspect them. We find them on an outcrop of rocks in a small meadow near some huts. The red figures of various animals on the flat surface of these large rocks are in very good condition even though they were painted by Bushmen centuries ago. Due to this being an out-of-the-way place, no visitors come around to see them, I am told.

We end up back in Kugombo Village and visit with Bero, who is the leader here. He is asked to also oversee

Murehwa District and to start new congregations there. I hand out some Bibles and tracts for him to give the new church leaders when a congregation has been planted. While we are waiting for the people to assemble for a service, his wife feeds us. It is after dark when we meet. Guni translates for me into Shona, a language spoken by most Zimbabweans. After the service I pray for those who seek physical healing. It is ten o'clock when I bunk down in the vehicle for the night. The front seat is my bed and the sleeping bag I brought along is my blanket.

I have a fairly good night. Woke up a few times though. I crawl out at six. The sun is already up. Looks like another hot day! It is nine o'clock before we are given a cup of tea. No food. I agree to assist the women financially in their project of raising chickens. Then, it is off to Matsenga Village for a service. There are approximately sixty who have gathered to hear us. After the message, many come forward wanting not salvation but healing! Rather unusual. The church committee is chosen and we pray before leaving for Harare.

Back in the city, I purchase more Bibles and songbooks in the Shona language. Also, buy a piece of black and white cloth that I am to give the chief of the area we are going to tomorrow. Finally, we stop at the EFZ office and give them a copy of our *Constitution and Bylaws*. Before I can call it a day, I drop off the ones who have been with me all day, and do a bit of shopping for the things that Marion wants me to bring her.

Up early. Four men are traveling with me down to the Zambezi Valley and visit the church in Kabvuma Village. It takes a little longer today because of missing the turn-off at Mvurwi. The ones who knew the route were quiet and so I kept driving. I finally checked the map when I noticed the scenery was not the same as last time.

Too far gone to turn back, so I kept going, taking another route. We come across countless villages and when I stop to ask about churches in this remote area, I am told there are none! I can see now that the Lord wanted us to miss the turn-off in order to show us this field to harvest for Him. I will have to send one of the men here to do some reaping!

Stafford, the pastor at Kabvuma Village, did not know that we were coming, but soon people started gathering under the big tree for a worship service. We are given tea and bread while we wait. Guni translates my message for me. The sick come forth for healing and one for demon oppression. After the service, we drive over to meet the chief. I give him his gifts, one of them being the two pieces of cloth I had bought in Harare. This custom of honoring the chief is quite rigid. While he is seated, those around him keep clapping their hands. He has a sore leg and asks me to pray for him. I do, with Stafford translating it into the chief's dialect.

There is another service tonight followed with prayer for those who have needs. Afterwards there is a time for questions, one of them being: "Is it permissible for a Christian to take home brew and place it on the grave of the parents, or relatives, in order to appease the departed spirits so that they will come back and live with them in peace?" This custom is still being practiced out here! It has not died out after all these years.

They go on to say that a chicken is sacrificed as well. A piece of cloth is tied to one leg and then the bird is dunked into the home brew until it is dead. This is supposed to appease the ancestral spirits. The end result is that the spirits come and dwell with them. No wonder then that many are possessed! The evil spirits impersonate the dead relatives and enter the homes of the living relatives and possess them. Because of this custom, they have unknowingly opened themselves to be invaded by demons.

It is ten o'clock before I get to bed. I sleep across the front seats of the Nissan. It is a warm night, so I am quite comfortable. In the morning there is tea and bread before we take off for Mashumbi Pools for a baptismal service. There are forty-five who are getting baptized. I also share on child dedication and end up praying for seventeen children and their parents. Some of the fathers are not present as so often is the case. We eat at the pastor's house before leaving for Harare. We arrive in the city late afternoon. After dropping off everyone, I turn in at the motel, have a hearty meal, take a bath in the tub, and climb into bed. Tomorrow I should be back in Lusaka by the end of the day.

Before I can leave Zimbabwe there is still one more service. This one is in someone's yard at a place called Zengeza, 30 kilometers south of Harare. About 40 have gathered in front of the house. I again preach and several come forward for prayer, some of them for salvation. No tree around, so I am standing out under the hot sun. When it is over, the top of my head actually feels like it got sunburned. Lungu and I leave at noon. We take along Bero as far as the Muriel Mines turn-off. He is to revive the work there. He has a son-in-law who works at the mines and is presently the leader of the church. We pray for him and continue on to Zambia.

We do not hold a service at Pembere, after we have crossed into Zambia. It is already too late in the day for that. Lungu informs me that the son of the pastor at Pembere is a poacher and is presently in jail. He was caught with the horns from four rhino in his possession, he and some of his friends had gotten them from across the border in Zimbabwe. We reach Lusaka at dark. I added 2,200 kilometers on the Nissan with this trip to Zimbabwe. Drop off Lungu at his house and then it is on to my home. Marion has been busy herself during my absence, putting up curtains and sorting out things in a container. We talk for some time, sharing what had transpired during our time apart before calling it a day.

Three
Strengthening Churches

Marion is accompanying me on this trip to Zimbabwe where we plan to spend a week in strengthening the churches and planting new ones. We reach the border in good time. On the Zambia side, the men in charge of the barrier each ask for a New Testament and some tracts. I consent. No questions are asked on the Zimbabwe side of the border about all the Bibles and tracts we were bringing into the country. At one o'clock, we stop alongside the road and eat the lunch that Marion has brought along.

When we reach Harare, we book in at the motel. I then drive out to check on Dzingai Guni. I find him and his wife living in a lean-to that is attached to someone's house. Nothing more than a one-room shack constructed out of sheets of corrugated metal sheets. Unbelievable! He directs me to a house in Rugare, a suburb of Harare, where they have started holding services. The occupant of this house is a boxer who, at one time, used to be the Bantamweight titleholder for Africa. His name is Sticks McLeod. In his match for the Commonwealth title, he lost to an Australian boxer. Sticks fought between the years 1980–1985. I have a short visit with him before we sing a couple of choruses. After prayer, Guni and I leave. We are to return tomorrow for a service.

Marion is with me when we go back to the boxer's

house. There are thirty-five of us squeezed inside one of the rooms for the service. Guni and his wife Monica are there. I preach and a dozen souls come forward for prayer, four of them for salvation. Pass out tracts to those present. It was a good service and I trust that they will carry on for the Lord. Guni will be shepherding them. It is dark when we arrive back to our lodging place.

In the morning of our third day here in Zimbabwe, we travel 300 kilometers south of Harare to Masvingo. I am finding that diesel is less than half the price it is in Zambia! We reach our destination at noon. Marion and I are remaining here to tour the nearby famous Greater Zimbabwe Ruins while Guni is going on to where we will have our service tomorrow and notify them of our coming. He used to live not far from here.

Marion and I check in at the motel just outside the ruins. After lunch we walk into the preserve and begin our inspection of the great walled enclosure that is the largest in sub-Sahara Africa. It is 250 meters in circumference with walls 11 meters high and 5 meters thick! It has three entrances and the interior is divided into compartments by inner walls. Two solid conical towers stand on the southern end. Nearby there are many smaller enclosures built out of stone where the villagers used to live. We climb up the cliff along a narrow path to view the hill complex, an enclosure built on top of the rocks. It is strongly fortified and protected by gigantic boulders. Like the circular structure below, the interior of this one up here is also divided into compartments. From one of these a stairway leads to a series of caves.

As to the dates of these ruins there is much difference of opinion. The guide informs us that they date back to the 11th and 12th centuries. But there are also those who think that this is the biblical Ophir from whence King

Solomon is said to have derived large quantities of precious metal. A very interesting hike! It is five o'clock when we get back to our room.

We leave for Museba Village in the morning and travel south 90 kilometers before we see Guni waiting beside the tarmac road. He guides us the rest of the way, another three kilometers along a path, to the village. About fifty people show up and we hold the service under a tree. Marion shares before I bring the message. Guni translates. Over twenty accept Christ into their hearts. Also pray for the sick and for those who want more power. Eleven children are dedicated. Bibles and tracts are distributed. There are several churches here already in Chivi District, due mainly to Guni's evangelistic efforts. The women serve us a big meal before our departure for Harare. When we reach the city, Guni gets off at his home and we carry on to our lodging place. It is now eight in the evening.

The following two days are spent shopping for supplies that the church here in Zimbabwe needs and meeting with the leaders so as to explain the *Constitution and Bylaws* to them, and what each one's duties are. Dzingai Guni finds a place that has two rooms available for rent. I tell him to take it and we will help him with the rent so that he and his wife can live in something better than where they are now. There is a Sunday service at Zengeza. We take along with us several members from the Rugare congregation, ending up with eleven adults and three children in our Nissan! The meeting is in a hall this time. Many have come and it is full. I preach and many come up for salvation, healing, and for spiritual strength. It is mid afternoon before we arrive back at the motel.

We are leaving Harare this Monday morning and

travel back to Lusaka after we do some shopping for groceries. At the shopping center we do not come across the two white men who had begged us for a loaf of bread sometime back. They have just disappeared. Surely, they were angels sent to test us. When we reach Cloud's End we pull in for a sandwich and a cup of tea. Sitting there we also drink in the scenic view around us—flowering trees, beautiful shrubs, and the distant purple hills.

This has become so much a part of our lives. We daydream and discuss the possibility of retiring in Africa since all of our children and grandchildren are living here. It would have to be Tanzania, Zambia, or Zimbabwe. This, of course, needs further prayer, looking into, and discussing it with our kids. We cross the border without any kind of delay and reach home safely. It's good to be back in our own home.

*　　*　　*

Ten weeks later Marion and I are back in Zimbabwe. We are again here for a week. Make my customary trip to the bank soon after our arrival for Zimbabwe dollars. The rate has been staying between seven and eight to a U.S. dollar. I spend some time discussing the work with Guni and Bero. It is stabilizing but not growing. Bero has not been traveling to the places he was asked to go. He keeps changing the program to suit himself. O, Lord, put some fire into the souls of these church leaders here in Zimbabwe! Can they not have the same passion for their own people as I have?

There is a service at a new place in Harare the day after our arrival. The people have gathered in a house. The room is full and it is difficult to pray for those who are seeking help after my message. It takes some time before we are through. The church leader here is a woman. Marion and I are both tired when we turn in tonight.

Up early, as today we are expected to hold a service at a new church in Mupozvori Village. To get there, we must travel down to Kadoma and then west 100 kilometers to Sinyati. After that, it is over a gravelled road and finally down a cow path. Guni and Bero are along. We find a woman is in charge here as well. Quite a few have gathered for the service that is being held under a tree. After my message, Marion and I pray for those who have come forward and are kneeling in the dust. We also pray for the pastor and her committee. They have prepared food for us consisting of chicken meat and *sadza*. Mealie meal here in Zimbabwe is called *sadza,* while in Zambia it is *nsima.*

When we are ready to leave, the Christians give us a live chicken, pumpkins, and groundnuts as gifts. What a generous group! Marion also receives some crocheted dollies and a crocheted tablecloth from the ladies for the used clothing she gave them. At Kadoma, Guni and Bero catch a bus back to Harare while we proceed down to Bulawayo. It is already dark when we reach the city. Tomorrow we will look at some of the historical sites before returning to Harare. This city is well known for its wide streets. At the museum, one finds the second-largest mounted elephant in the world! (The largest is at the Nairobi Museum.)

Back in Harare while parked downtown on one of the streets, two men approach us and demand to see the logbook and entry permit from Customs. We smell crooks and refuse. They persist and one of them produces an ID (identity card) from Customs when I ask for one. I comply and show him the documents. They then leave. I go on to meet with Guni and Bero, and to purchase Bibles and a bike for the Murehwa district chairman. Meanwhile Marion asks at a shop whether customs officials would walk around checking on vehicles like that? She was told that they were crooks sizing up our vehicle since it has Zambian license plates. No officials work on Saturdays, especially on the streets. Our prayer tonight is that the Lord will protect our vehicle while here in Harare.

I leave Marion behind and drive out to Murehwa District for a service at a new place. She needs to rest up her back that has been paining her because of much traveling. Dzingai Guni and his wife, plus Bero, are coming along to Chikuhwa Village. It is situated five kilometers off the tarmac road. A good thing Marion is not along as it is very rough going. Arrive in plenty of time, but then we end up waiting three hours for the service to begin! The women serve us chicken, *sadza*, and corn-on-the-cob during this time.

There are forty-two who finally show up for the service. Guni translates my message and quite a few come up for salvation and for healing. There is also a young woman who is possessed by two ancestral spirits. The demons are strong and it takes four of us to hang onto her so that they cannot drag her away. The demons do not want to give up their host! I am told she has her grandmother's ancestral spirit. Omitting a loud shriek, it is the first one to leave. I then command the last demon to give its name and promptly receive a blow on my mouth! It keeps on refusing to give me its name. So I let up and concentrate on driving it out. Finally, the demon says in the Shona language, "I'm going!" and leaves the woman. It took us all of fifteen minutes to drive them both out.

When we finally get back to Harare, I return the Gunis to their place and carry on to the motel. Before I reach it, I mail my granddaughter, Tiffany, in Uganda, a postcard of Zimbabwe. I send her one from each of the countries that I travel to. Marion still needs to do some shopping, so we'll do that yet this evening. Tomorrow we return to Lusaka and home.

*   *   *

After spending a few months visiting the churches in Zambia, we are again back in Zimbabwe. This time Marion and I are on our way to Masvingo Province. Guni and Bero are traveling with us. We will be spending the night at the town of Masvingo and then tomorrow carry on for another 100 kilometers further south till we reach the village of Chiramba, where a service is planned for us.

It is a small village nestled in among hills that have large boulders along the top as if someone stacked them. We had to drive a considerable distance to get here. The Lord did say that we are to go to the ends of the earth! This is one of those spots. At least 150 people show up for the service. They appear out of the bush from all around us. Amazing! Marion shares and I bring the message. Many come forward for salvation. It is a very good meeting. They serve us chicken, rice, and *sadza* before we start our return trip. We give the district leader a ride to Masvingo and there we purchase a bicycle for him to use in visiting the churches as there already are over seven of them in his district.

The following morning we leave for the Zambezi Valley and reach Kabvuma Village at noon. It is very hot and dry here. Stafford thought we were coming tomorrow and so no one is ready for us. His wife feeds us, including the two men we brought with us—Guni and Bero. While waiting for the people to arrive for the evening service, I give

Guni his TEE test in the fourth book, *The Shepherd and His Work*. He does okay.

There is no moon out during our service tonight. About thirty-five villagers are present. When I finish my message, two come forward for prayer saying that they are sick. But when I begin praying for the first one, demons start manifesting themselves. I drive two traditional spirits from her, but there is yet a third demon inside. It is a dumb spirit and it won't speak. Finally, the woman herself says that the demons are all gone, and then adds that they are waiting for her at home. She takes off running with a demon shouting, "Why are we being chased away?" The woman must have charms and fetishes at her hut that are keeping her bound. It is too dark to follow her. But, will she return tomorrow to receive complete victory?

Marion and I are sleeping in Stafford's house tonight. The bed is narrow and we are finding it difficult to drop off to sleep. There is nothing much of a mattress and the springs are bothering Marion. Meanwhile the grain dust from the bags of maize and the smell from the bales of cotton in the room are giving me hay fever. At ten o'clock, we have had enough of it and move outside to sleep in the Nissan. Marion takes the front seats and I take the ones behind her. It isn't comfortable as we cannot stretch out our legs but at least we have clean air to breathe. At six in the morning, we get dressed before crawling out of the vehicle.

The service begins at nine o'clock and sixty villagers show up under the tree. Marion again shares before my message. Afterwards we pray for those seeking help. A sick child with a charm around her neck is brought up for healing by the mother. When asked to remove it, the mother says that she can't until the husband agrees. He is not present at the service as he is still a pagan. Will the Lord still hear our prayer? Until the charm is removed, the mother who is a Christian is told that the Lord will not heal her child.

After the service a meeting is held to choose a chairman for the district. There are now eight churches here in Guruve District; one of them is at Kanyemba, near the Zambezi River. Just across the river is our church at Luangwa, Zambia, and another one at Zumbo, Mozambique. (Three countries converge at this point along the banks of the Zambezi River.) We give the new committee money to purchase mealie meal for the famine-stricken families in the area. Stafford's wife feeds us before we take off for Muriel Mines where there will be a service this evening.

It is mid afternoon when we reach Muriel Mines. After supper there is a meeting with about thirty in attendance. Pray for several after my sermon. We are sleeping in a house that has a bed with springs so soft that Marion and I roll together most of the night. In the morning there is another service with thirty-five people present. Marion shares and we sing a duet before I preach from the Word of God. We help those asking for prayer. Then it is time to leave and return to Lusaka. Along the way, Guni and Bero drop off at the main road and catch a bus back to Harare.

When we reach home, Marion and I discover water on the floor from a leaky toilet bowl in the spare bathroom. Marion also finds the pantry infested with weevils. They have come from the beans that were stored there. So we still have work to do before we can retire for the night.

*　　*　　*

Our next trip to visit the churches in Zimbabwe finds us crossing the border at Livingstone. Here, a bridge spans the Zambezi River connecting Zambia to Zimbabwe. From it, we catch a magnificent view of mighty Victoria Falls! We are now in the small tourist town of Victoria Falls, once known as Fort Victoria. Cash some money into the local currency and carry on to Bulawayo, 450 kilometers south. At the Safari Lodge, situated beside the Hwange National Park, we stop for a bite to eat. There is a waterhole here for the animals and we watch the elephants and several other species of wildlife for a spell before resuming our safari.

When we reach Bulawayo, Guni is waiting for us. Our plan to remain here for the weekend to plant a couple of churches has been changed, he informs us. We are to travel to Kadoma tomorrow and then on to Sinyati District. I was looking forward to a break of at least one day before traveling a long distance again. This driving of long distances is taking its effect on me. My neck is sore and I feel exhausted. Marion gives me a massage which helps some. I need a good night of rest so I turn in early.

There is a service at someone's house before we can leave Bulawayo. Thirty people have gathered to hear me preach. It is translated into Ndebele, the language of the people here in and around Bulawayo. Marion helps those who come forward to pray. We are fed chicken and rice before setting off for Kadoma. Guni is traveling with us. It is getting dark when we arrive so we decide to spend the night here in town.

In the morning, we move along and reach Makwechere Village, situated in Sinyati District, without a problem. It is deep in the dry countryside. The service is held in front of some huts where approximately fifty villagers have gathered. The church leader is a woman recently appointed by Guni. Marion again assists me with praying for the sick and the lost after my message. They feed us chicken and *sadza* after the service is over.

The chicken that we ate was alive when we arrived. Marion and I saw three girls chasing a hen that still had small chicks trailing along behind her. The smallest of the three girls finally caught the hen. The head was promptly cut off and then the feathers plucked. We watched the whole drama unfold from where we sat. By the time the service had finished, the chicken was cooked and ready for us to eat.

Marion hands out used clothing to the women and children. She buys some crocheted items from the women. The women in Zimbabwe are noted for their beautifully crocheted tablecloths and bedspreads that they sell for a living. We reach Harare before dark and take Guni home before we book in at a motel.

This morning I am traveling to Mutoko District where some new churches have been started. Marion is staying behind to do some shopping. I pick up the two national leaders, Guni and Bero, plus two other men who want to go along. Thirty kilometers beyond Mutoko town, I turn off and drive south a further 25 kilometers over a stony road before reaching our destination. The village of Chatidza is tucked away among the large rocks and boulders that litter the countryside. There are twenty-five or so present to hear the Word of God. Almost all of them want prayer and it takes me some time, as I do them one by one.

On my way back, Bero and his friends remain in Mutoko while Guni comes all the way to Harare. Marion has bought me a plate of fruit for Valentine's Day. I bombed out because of being busy all day with the trip into the bush and sharing the Word of God. I wrapped up

400 kilometers! All the nice eating places in the city are booked, so we can't go out. We end up eating here in the motel. It turns out to be a special Valentine's Day meal. Great!

We are returning to Zambia today. On the way, though, we are holding one more service before leaving Zimbabwe. Guni and his wife Monica have come with us. Near Karoi we turn east and drive 25 kilometers more until we reach the village of Nyama. Here we find only about twenty-five present for the service out of the one hundred and forty that we were told worship here on Sundays. Four churches have been opened here, Guni informs me. After the message most of them come forward for prayer. Marion and I leave right after the service. Guni and his wife are remaining behind to visit with her parents. Her father blew his kudu horn for the group that sang for us earlier in the service. Did a good job of it! He is the church leader here.

Instead of driving through Chirundu, we take the route back to Zambia through Kariba. Ten kilometers down the road from the turn-off at Cloud's End, we have a flat on one of the front tires. We drive without a spare the rest of the way home. The border crossing today was the quickest ever as we were the only ones. It's not like Chirundu where we have had to wait for an hour at times. It is common to find lorries (trucks) lined up a kilometer long waiting to have their loads processed. During this time baboons wander among the vehicles and on top of them, sniffing out those that carry maize. When they locate them, they rip holes into the sacks and help themselves to its contents.

Zimbabwe—the land of stones

Rock paintings by early Bushmen

The ancient Greater Zimbabwe Ruins

Marion hands out sacks of mealie meal.

Inside the Greater Zimba-
bwe Ruins

Unusual rock formations
scattered about

Marion and brother Jerry
with his daughter Cindy

Pounding maize into flour

Plowing their fields with oxen

Digging holes and planting maize

Here are truckloads of maize for the famine stricken.

Food is distributed to needy household members.

Teaching a class in front of their huts

Dzingai Guni receives his ordination.

Many services are held under trees in Zimbabwe.

A worshipper is blowing the horn from a kudu.

Mozambique border post at Cassacatiza

Office of Minister of Religious Affairs, Maputo

Destroyed tank from the recent civil war

Marion and railway cars blown off the tracks

The battery blew up because of high temperatures.

The goat must travel on top with the luggage!

A tube gets patched along a lonely road.

The *Macuta* foundered on the beach at Beira.

One cot with a mosquito net

Booking in at guesthouse in Mutarara

Bridge spanning Zambezi River at Mutarara/Sena

This latrine sits on a termite mound.

The Zambezi River floods all the low areas.

Tents are put up for the homeless and displaced people.

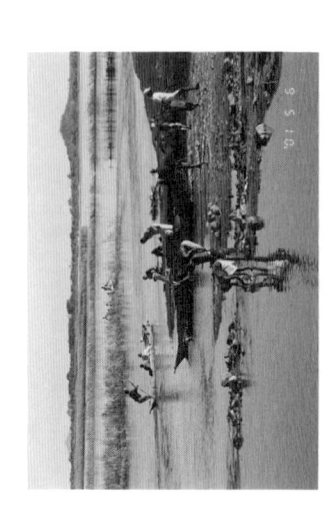

Assisting flood victims with food and bikes

Marion receives a chicken as a gift from Christian.

Musical instruments are also made from bicycle parts.

One of the congregations at Beira

Pebble-filled cans serve as musical instruments.

Delivering the Word of God

Colleen, Mario, and Reinhard share in service.

Colleen stands in the market place at Sena.

One of many churches in Mozambique

Reinhard, Colleen, Thomas, Mario, and Isai at Tete

Four
Traveling Limitations

On our following trip, we meet with the Executive Committee at Guni's house in Harare. They have all showed up today May 19, 1995, for the meeting. After everyone has read their reports, we discover there are now 103 churches in Zimbabwe with over 4,200 members. Praise the Lord! I pass out the Bibles and tracts I brought with me from Lusaka. It has been a good day.

The next day we again meet at Guni's place, this time to hold our Executive Council meeting. I take time to answer their questions concerning the *Constitution and Bylaws*. Several write their TEE tests afterwards. I purchase two bicycles, one for the chairman at Karoi District and the other one for the chairman at Guruve District. Another full day!

We meet for the third time in as many days. Today we have a worship service where twenty-six are present to witness the ordination of Dzingai Guni and to observe the ordinances of Communion and Foot Washing. It is an all around good service. Guni is representing Zimbabwe at the 1995 World Conference held in Australia this time. Lungu is going as well to represent Zambia. Marion gives out used clothing to those who are in need of them. Our passion for African souls has brought the church thus far these past three years in Zimbabwe.

The work continues to expand in Zimbabwe as it reaches out into the countryside. I try to keep up with it and drive to as many new areas as I can on each visit I make. The responsibility of overseeing the work in Southern Africa is increasing continually. More laborers and funds are needed to not only reach out even more with the gospel but to stabilize what already has been started.

Is there no one else besides Marion and me who is interested in planting churches here in Zimbabwe, Mozambique, Malawi, and yes, Angola? Where in Canada and the States is the passion for souls in faraway Africa? Is it entirely our responsibility because we said, "Here am I, Lord, send me"? The Apostle Paul had Timothy and Titus. Whom do we have? Missionaries are needed to assist us in teaching, preaching, and raising funds for literature, bicycles, and building projects here in Southern Africa! Is there no one to share my passion for Africa?

In spite of my heavy schedule in Zambia, I continue to visit the work in Zimbabwe. I again take relief to the churches in the Zambezi Valley, in Murehwa, Chivi, and Sinyati Districts, where there is widespread famine due to no rain during planting season. Women and children must carry water from the distant riverbeds. Their only mistake is that they were born poor! I preach and teach the Word to those who gather under the trees, but without compassion for their physical needs it sounds empty and void. "Lord, help me to ever be a vessel of your love and mercy. Let me never become calloused. As much as you pour out into my hands, I will pass it on to the poor, the needy, and the suffering here in Africa." Amen.

There is a great need to enlighten the people on ancestral spirits as many are oppressed and possessed by them. Every opportunity I have I am teaching them that it is the devil's way to use their belief in these spirits to oppress them and finally to enter and possess them. Because we do not live here in Zimbabwe so as to visit our churches more often, there are not as many people delivered from demon possession as we have had take place in Zambia. The national leaders are not as eager in getting involved with the deliverance ministry. Once they get stronger in the Word and put on the whole armor of God, I am sure they will.

On one trip as I am checking in at the motel in Harare, I discover that my credit card and U.S. dollars are not in my case! I have left them on my desk in the office back home. All I have with me is Zambia Kwacha, about six hundred dollars' worth. They will not accept the Kwacha at the desk. The banks are already closed for the day so I try the Forex Bureaus, but they will not change the Zambia Kwacha into Zimbabwe dollars. This is a real problem when traveling from country to country in most of Africa; they will not accept each other's currencies. Therefore, I must always travel with U.S. dollars or British pounds in order to buy their local currencies. Even the Canadian dollar cannot help you. Credit cards are honored at banks in most countries, if you catch them during working hours.

I return to the motel and after explaining my dilemma to the manager, he books me in for the night. At eight in the morning, I am at the bank to see if they will change my Kwacha into their currency. They refuse. They send me to check with Aero Zambia, but they could not assist me either. I am told to try the Zambian High Commission. No success as well. A last resort is the Canadian High Commission. After hearing my predicament, the receptionist calls Kim, our daughter-in-law who works at the Canadian High Commission in Lusaka, for proof of identification. She talks to me on the phone as well and informs me that there is a $250 emergency fund that people in distress are given. The commissioner finally steps out of his office and tells me in his French accent that I do not qualify for this assistance!

All my talking does not budge him—even though I promised to pay it back as soon as I return to Lusaka. Is this the kind of man they send out to represent Canada? All the help I have rendered to others and now when there is an opportunity to be rendered onto with a bit of charity, I am denied by a fellow Canadian! What irony! I wonder if it would have made a difference if I had come unkempt, wearing sandals, and tattered trousers instead of looking well dressed?

I am now forced to try the outdoor market and find someone there who is willing to change my Kwacha into the local currency. I remain behind in the motel while Guni goes to the marketplace. As a white stranger I would attract too much attention, I am told. He returns with approximately a hundred dollars' worth, enough to pay for the room and fuel to take us to the border. I then leave for Lusaka taking Guni with me. We reach home and there I find the credit cards and U.S. dollars on my desk where I had forgotten them. I surprise everyone with my quick return. Guni is going back to Harare in the morning with money to carry on until my return to Zimbabwe in three weeks.

*   *   *

On this trip, Marion is traveling with me. It is a year ago today that Kirk's wife Karen had her fatal accident. It is still very difficult for us to accept that this tragic event took place. There is a meeting with the national leaders here in Harare tomorrow and it will be held at the Red Cross Training Center.

We are able to start at nine o'clock. There are eleven of us. The meeting went well and we conclude at four in the afternoon. When I return to the motel, I find Marion being questioned by a policeman. After he leaves, she explains that when she was returning on foot from the nearby shopping center, three men mugged her and got away with her handbag! She did not know that they were following her until one grabbed her around the neck from behind. A second one then snatched the handbag, tearing it from her arm. The third man shoved her roughly to the sidewalk. Just then a red Benz pulled up and the three scrambled inside and sped away. It all happened so quickly!

A Zimbabwean woman standing in front of her house saw it all happen and came over to assist Marion back to the motel. Marion is thoroughly shaken from the rough treatment she has just experienced. The three muggers may have robbed her of more items had it not been for a vehicle, coming up the street, which scared them off. The driver gave chase but lost them. He, as it turns out, is staying here in the motel.

Marion did not have much money in her handbag. But she did have a credit card that now needs to be cancelled. I call the company in the States and it takes some time to get it done. Men from the CID (Criminal Investigation Department) show up and interview Marion about the theft. It is a busy evening! When we finally get to our room, we have prayer. Marion has several bruises on her neck where she was choked, and on her arm from the strap of the handbag when the thief tore it from her. It could have been much worse.

The following day is Sunday so we attend the service

here in Harare at the Rugare congregation. Marion gives her testimony of how she was mugged, and how the Lord protected her from greater danger. I present Guni with his First Course Certificate in the TEE program for completing the first twelve books. We pray for those who come up for prayer after my message. Before we can leave for Lusaka, there are a few more things I need to purchase for the work here in Zimbabwe.

We park on a side street and I walk with the district chairmen to hunt for bicycles that they need for evangelism. It is raining heavily, so Marion remains in the vehicle with the doors locked and the windows turned up. While I am gone, someone comes up to the window and tries to coax her to step outside by saying that there is a fire under the Nissan! Now where did Marion hear something like this before? Did they really think she was that naive? She refuses and another man joins him and says that they want to change some money. Time to bring this to an end, so Marion pushes down on the horn and keeps it there until they walk away. No bystander offers to come to her aid! And it all takes place in front of a shop. Imagine!

Today, November 17, 1996, is the third day that Rwandans are on the move back to their homeland from Zaire. It is an unbelievable sight, to watch this mass of humanity trudging along the dusty road from Goma to Gisenyi. About half a million refugees have already returned to Rwanda and more on the way! No one expected this huge exodus. Where all this is taking place, is very familiar to me. I used to travel there while in Uganda overseeing the work in Zaire and Rwanda. It is difficult to hold back the tears as we watch on TV the children and old people struggling to keep up with the others. Some of the very young get separated from their mothers and are swallowed up in the flight to freedom. Will they ever be reunited again? O, the horrors of war!

*   *   *

On one of my last trips to Zimbabwe with the Nissan, I drive down to Masvingo through Bulawayo as we are now residing in Livingstone and not Lusaka. I am discovering there is a shortage of fuel here in Zimbabwe and it takes me a while finding a station that has any. I book in a motel at Masvingo and wait for Guni to show up. When he does, we make plans for tomorrow. When it's time to turn in, I discover that I again have forgotten my towel! How many times is that now? I sleep well.

In the morning I run through some of my back-and-stomach exercises before taking a bath. I need to keep fit for all my travels. Pick up some local currency at the bank with my credit card and then purchase a towel and fuel for the Nissan. They have kerosene here so I mix it with the diesel. I have been doing this for several years, as it is supposed to be cleaner on the motor.

When I reach Ngundu, I order 150 bags of maize for distribution to the needy at Chiramba Village. A lorry will bring them out Monday, two days from now. Guni and I carry on ten more kilometers east and then a short distance south along a trail to where there had been a landslide during the heavy rains in February. Huge boulders on top of the rocky ridge had come crashing down ripping up trees and rocks along its path. A miracle that no lives were lost! Just a few houses were destroyed. The mud and rocks stopped just at the village's edge. It's quite a sight! A deep ravine-like depression has been carved into the mountainside. It did the same thing on the other side of the ridge.

I cross the road and drive to Chiramba Village. I have been here before. At noon I am not served any food, so I snack on what I have brought with me. I learn that one of the men here died of AIDS recently. The service is after dark tonight as the villagers work all day in their fields. It is planting time. Rain is threatening and there is much lightning during the singing and preaching. No lights are necessary as the lightning is continuous. I make it through my sermon and into the Nissan before it begins to pour. There is a great deal of wind with the rain. The lightning appears to flash horizontally and not vertically! I have never seen it like this before. Very eerie! I watch it from inside my vehicle until it rumbles off into the distance. It is then that I am able to drop off to sleep.

There is a second rainstorm in the middle of the night that awakens me. It is a repeat of the first one with continuous horizontal flashes of lightning. The thunder is not as loud, a bit more muffled. I manage to go back to sleep again and finish the night on the front seats. In the morning Guni reports that the wind blew off some roofs during the night. I walk out to look at some of them. There are no latrines here in the village. I, therefore, am careful where I step as I make my way about. Guni informs me that there is actually one person here who has an outhouse and he takes me to it. It is one kilometer away from where I am parked!

The people here are very lazy and inhospitable! I was not served lunch or supper yesterday. Even when I was visiting Guni at the district chairman's hut and found the wife and children eating corn-on-the-cob, she would not offer me any. Today, while inspecting the damage done by last night's rainstorm, it begins to shower and we enter a hut. The occupants are eating but do not offer us any of their food. If this were Zambia, they would have invited us to join them. I do not know whether the villagers here think that I do not eat with the Africans, or they really are inhospitable? I talk to Guni about this. Finally, the woman of the hut near to where I am parked brings Guni and me tea and some bread that tastes of wood smoke.

The Sunday service is held under some trees. At least 140 have come to hear the Word of God. The women do a lot of ululating during the singing and, when I stand up to preach, I ask them what it means? They answer me that it is an expression of joy. I spend some time teaching from the Bible before delivering the sermon. Many of them want me to pray for them after the message. There is a break before the next service begins. During this time Guni and I are fed rice and chicken by the chairman's wife. The rest of the congregation sit around, or go behind the anthills and bushes to answer the call of nature. Remember, no outhouses!

Many come up for special prayer after my second message. One of them is an old woman with a bottle containing tobacco tied around her neck. I remove it before praying for her. All in all, it has been a good day in the Word. For supper we are served rice, chicken, and corn-on-the-cob. The women are doing better today! Guni must have had a little talk with them. I again sleep in the Nissan with my sleeping bag. It's a bit cramped on the front seats but it beats a hut getting bitten all night by mosquitoes.

This morning I do not take a shower in the grass enclosure as I did yesterday, but take only a shave with the warm water brought to me. Walk out to the latrine and find the villagers already out in their fields at six. Some are using oxen or donkeys to pull the plows. Still others are hoeing by hand. They are planting maize and groundnuts. At eight, Guni and I drive to Ngundu to find out why the lorry had not yet arrived with the maize I had purchased two days ago.

I discover nothing is moving, so we hire one quickly and the driver begins transporting the bags to Miramba Village. He has to make two trips to fetch all the 150 sacks, each one weighing 50 kilos. It is mid afternoon before all the maize gets distributed to the 70 families that have come from several nearby villages. It all went very peacefully, each one taking his or her turn. When all is done, Guni and I take off for Masvingo. From there he goes on to Chinhoyi where he now lives with his family.

I spend the night in Masvingo and wake up with malaria and have to postpone my trip back to Livingstone. I have severe chills that wreck my body something fierce. Then after the chills, a high fever sets in. I stay in bed all day and take Arinate to get rid of my malaria. By morning I am still weak but start off for home anyway. It is a 900-kilometer safari and I make it without a mishap. The Lord kept me awake all the way. Thank you!

*   *   *

My plan to make another trip into the countryside in order to visit churches does not take place. The political situation in Zimbabwe is hotting up (as the Zambians would say), making it ever too risky to drive a vehicle off the beaten track. The newspapers are full of articles of President Mugabe and his so-called war veterans invading land belonging to white farmers. Another white Zimbabwean, an eighty-year-old woman, was shot and killed on her farm. No one is being brought to justice for any of the killings. It has become a racial situation and highly inflammatory! The world stands by and watches.

There is a fuel shortage in Harare, not to mention the

smaller towns, where long queues are lined up at the few filling stations that may have some petrol. This country is rapidly coming apart at the seams. I, therefore, choose to fly into Harare instead and meet with Guni to discuss the future of the work. During this time, I also meet with Chomanika who hurries in from Malawi. He is flying on to London to attend the World Conference where he will represent Malawi. Chitui was to have gone as well to represent Mozambique, but he got turned back at the Zimbabwe border.

For my last trip to Zimbabwe, Marion flies with me to Harare. It is August 31, 2001. A friend drives us to the border, and after passing through Immigration and Customs, we hire a taxi that takes us to the small airport several miles outside the town of Victoria Falls. The flight departs at 3:30 P.M. and an hour later we disembark at the Harare airport. Kirk is there to pick us up and we drive to his house. UNICEF (United Nations International Children's Emergency Fund) moved him and his family to Harare from Lusaka the beginning of the year. The girls have grown since the last time we saw them. Mikaela has changed the most. Even so, she is still Opa's little girl. At the supper table, she wants me to sit beside her. Her birthday was several days ago but they waited for us. There is a birthday cake and gifts afterwards. It is midnight before we turn in.

Kirk and Suzie drop me off in town where I meet Guni, who has come in from Chinhoyi to supply me the latest report on the work here in Zimbabwe. Marion is remaining behind with Kirk, when I fly on to Malawi and spend two days with Paffett Chomanika gathering the latest reports of the church in that country. The plane leaves for Blantyre at 1:30 P.M. It is an aircraft with propellers and is not a jet. The air conditioners are not working, so it is a hot and humid flight of one and a half hours! No one complains, so I don't either. Chomanika is at the airport when I arrive.

My return flight to Harare is with the same plane and I discover the air conditioners are still not functioning. It is again a hot ride! This aircraft has seen its better days. It is coming apart at the seams. I have to knock the panel on the wall beside me back into its place! The humming of the engine just outside my seat is deafening. There is also a kid, as big around as he is tall, who screeches all the way to Harare! Marion and Suzie are there to pick me up at the airport. We spend the rest of the day with the family and visit until late. Tomorrow we fly back to Victoria Falls and then on to Livingstone by road.

Since March 1992, I have been their missionary but this role comes to an end when Marion and I retire from active service on July 1, 2002. I will meet Dzingai Guni one more time when he comes to our farewell in December of this year. I wish I could have made more trips to assist the church and strengthen the leaders, but then there are only so many days in a month. My schedule has always been full, traveling to one country or another. Because no one comes to my assistance, the Lord keeps renewing my strength to carry the load. My passion for Zimbabwe still burns as it did when I first began the work in 1992.

Mozambique

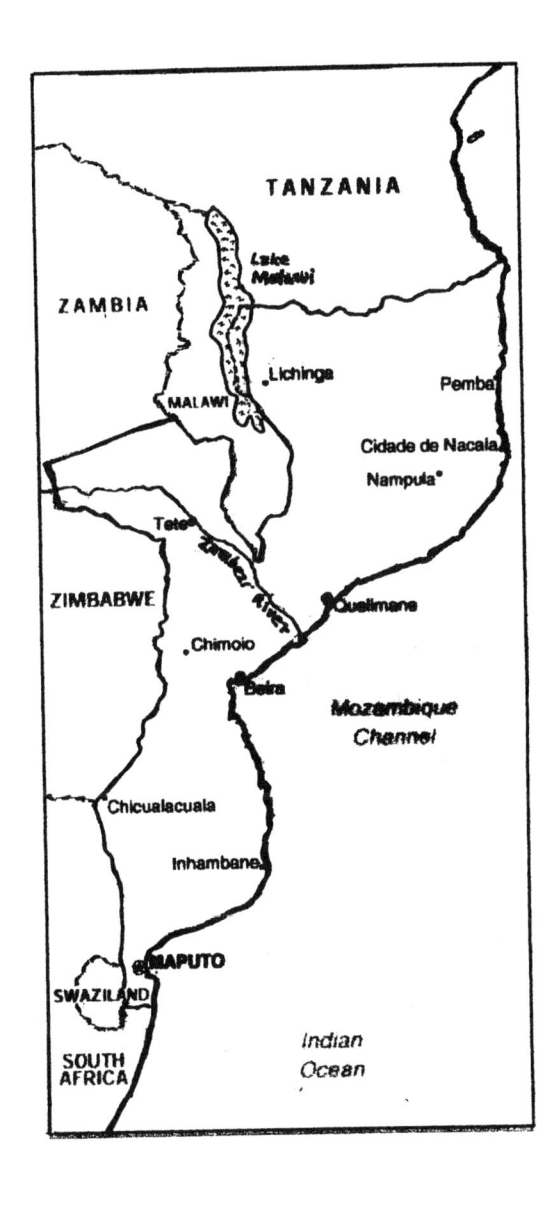

Five
Venturing into Mozambique

When finally in 1994 it is declared safe to take a vehicle across the border into Mozambique, so long as you keep to the main roads, I venture in with the gospel. There are still countless land mines scattered throughout the countryside with experts still in the process of removing them, but it is time to go. My first look at Mozambique is in June when Marion and Robert Edwards, the director for Africa, are with me. We had come from Malawi on our way to Zimbabwe and stopped at Tete for two nights. Because we had as yet no contacts, we could not do much more than just look around in the shops. Any contacts that we do have are villagers scattered along the border with Zambia.

On a trip in November 1994, I am prepared to do more than just look at shops. I take along Lungu to assist me with translation as where we are going in northern Mozambique many of them understand Nyanja. In fact, I am carrying with me Nyanja Bibles, as no Portuguese Bibles were available at any of the shops in Lusaka. It is noon when we reach Katete and find there is no electricity in town. How will I get diesel with no power at the pumps? One of the attendants at the filling station says he has some at his house. Now where did he get it? I buy enough to fill up the Nissan. Then I turn off the Great

East Road and travel 55 kilometers south to the border of Mozambique.

The Zambian officials are relaxed and we pass without a problem. The Mozambican border post appears deserted as we approach the barrier. It is small mud and wattle hut with a tarp for the roof. Very primitive! There are two men inside and no one speaks English but, fortunately for me, one of them speaks Swahili. Very unusual! We converse for some time. I am able to purchase $150 worth of Mozambican money, called Meticais, from him. This will help until I get more in the town of Tete.

The road is quite empty of life along the way. During the civil war the countryside had been completely vacated by the villagers. The buildings we come across have been ruined by shellfire. No cattle or goats, only a dog here and there trailing along behind his master. What I see reminds me of the days when we lived in Uganda. It is all too similar with what we encountered during the civil war in that country. We finally reach the Zambezi River that flows between the towns of Matundo and Tete. A long bridge spans the river and we cross it to get into Tete. It is hot and humid here. Even the wind is hot. We book into the Zambesi Hotel, as I did on my previous trip with Marion and Bob Edwards. There are a lot of UN (United Nations) personnel swarming around the place.

The Zambesi Hotel is supposed to be a five-star hotel but it hardly is fit to be a one-star. The water does not run all day, the sink is plugged, and the electricity goes off at certain hours. The hotel is in great disrepair but at one time it must have been a special place with its marble floors for Portuguese travelers during the colonial days. Lungu and I are the only ones eating supper in the dining room. There is just beef stew on the menu so we order it. Bata, our contact person here in Tete, finally shows up and we talk about getting the church registered here in Mozambique. His English is not that great. It is late so we plan to meet again tomorrow. No water for a bath tonight, so I have some brought up. I am all clammy from this high humidity.

There actually is warm water in the tap this morning, enough for a shave. Our breakfast is tea and bread. There is a large presence of UN workers in the hotel; they are using many of the rooms for their office work. The street outside is lined with their vehicles. They are presently distributing food to the refugees that have moved back from Zambia where they had fled to during the civil war. The UN has erected temporary camps for them to stay in until they are able to fend for themselves.

I am able to get more local currency. I get over 6,000 Meticais to a U.S. dollar! When Bata makes his appearance, I have him take us to see the Minister of Justice and Religious Affairs. There we are told what we need to do in order to have our church registered. It will take another trip or so to meet all their requirements. We are kept busy with paperwork until evening. The air conditioner in my room is working and so I have a good night's rest.

In the forenoon, it being Saturday, I check the shops and discover prices are cheaper here than in Zambia for some things. Diesel is half the price! At noon we gather at Bata's home and we are served *nsima, kapenta* (dried minnows), ochre, and groundnut sauce. After the meal, I teach those that have come for two hours. Then Lungu and I return to the hotel. From a window in the dining room, I watch four goats getting loaded onto the roof rack of a minibus. The animals are objecting to the rough treatment they are receiving. But finally the job is completed, the goats are standing alongside the luggage, and away they go down the street. The water comes on for a couple of hours tonight. It was on, as well, this morning for two hours. The rest of the day it is off.

I wake up to clear skies. Another hot day! Bata and his friends take Lungu and myself to a church they used to attend. In the service there is real pandemonium; drums beaten with large sticks, lots of dancing, and women ululating. After the bishop's message, many come forward and six of them manifest demon-possession. Those who are assisting them in front do not cast out the demons. In fact, they treat the possessed as having been filled with the Holy Spirit! None of the workers have the gift of discernment. One of the possessed has a religious spirit that keeps saying, "Naught! Naught! Naught!" I have heard this before from the possessed in Zambia. Being a stranger, I do not take part in their service.

After eating at Bata's home, I again teach the group. This time I share on testing the spirits, whether they are of the Lord or not. In the evening there is a service and after my message, I pray for many of them one by one. Cast out a religious spirit from one possessed person and from another one who was oppressed by them. There is a business meeting yet before Lungu and I return to the hotel for the night. It's been an unusual day. I even cut open my forehead, in two places, on the roofing sheets as I was coming out of Bata's house. I didn't duck far enough. It bled quite a bit.

Up early as today we return to Zambia. Meet with Bata and his friends before breakfast concerning the registration of the church. Then at ten o'clock, Lungu and I cross the long bridge over the Zambezi River and leave the town of Tete behind us. As we travel toward the border, we again pass the village where three tanks had been left behind during the civil war. As well, we come across the burned-out armored vehicles strewn alongside the road. Reminds me of those warring days in Uganda where relics of the civil war are still found beside the roads! No problem at the border.

*   *   *

On my next trip to Mozambique, I enter from Malawi. Lungu is along and so is Joash, a church leader in Blantyre. After crossing the border, we drive five kilometers to the village of one of our contacts here in Mozambique. I learn from him that he and Bata have returned to their previous church. They probably had never left the other group but had wanted to play both for what they could get. Too bad, now we have to start with new leaders again. It is mid afternoon when we arrive in Tete. We check in at Pescina this time. It is a rundown motel situated next to the bridge and managed by a Portuguese couple. Nothing much for sleeping quarters but it has a better menu than the Zambesi Hotel. We are told that the UN has pulled out most of its workers from Tete. It is again very hot and humid here.

The rooms here are small but they do have air conditioners, albeit they are old and very noisy. Lungu and Joash are able to retrieve all the documents from Bata and, after breakfast, set out on a mission to find new church leaders. When they return in the afternoon, they bring along two men who are interested to assist us. One of them is Manuel Chitui, who works in one of the banks here in Tete. The other one is Ezerone, a friend of his. I feel good about them and plan to resume working on the church registration with them tomorrow.

The sun is burning hot today. The temperature must be close to 50 degrees Celsius, that's about 120 degrees Fahrenheit! I was able to get some local currency from the moneychangers on the street. They are on every corner, with their hands full of foreign money from various countries. The worth of their currency is steadily declining.

The morning starts immediately with a scorching hot sun! We check about a post office box and are given one. Buy a couple of postcards and mail them, one to Tiffany and one to Ashling. Worked some more on the documents for the registration. In the afternoon we cross the bridge and hold a service in Matundo. There are over seventy in attendance. I preach and do some teaching afterwards. Hand out Bibles and tracts before we return to the motel. We eat our meal in the restaurant. It has been a good day.

The air conditioner in my room is not good for me, as I am coming down with a head cold. Take the men with me to the office of the Registrar where they talk again about the church registration. It is a very hot day. My thermometer shows 109 Fahrenheit! A wind comes up in the afternoon and stirs up quite a bit of dust. A light shower that amounts to nothing follows it. There are girls that hang around here in the evening. One of them comes knocking at my door and I hear an employee nearby tell her that I am a padre. She is embarrassed and promptly leaves. One other European had to call security tonight to drag away the girl from his door.

I am up at six this morning. Did a lot of perspiring during the night because I had switched off the air conditioner due to my sniffles. Our work here is done for this trip so we bid farewell to Chitui and his friends. Lungu and I then head for Zambia while Joash catches the bus back to Malawi. After we cross the border into Zambia, we stop for a service at Tiyese in Chadiza District. There is rain here but it stops when we begin the service and does not resume until we are in the vehicle ready to leave. A miracle! I have been given gifts to take home: two live pigeons, watermelons, maize, and rape (spinach). I reach home just at dark. Marion fared well during my absence.

*   *   *

When I return to Mozambique, Marion is with me this time. I again enter from Malawi at the border town of Zobue. We take along Joash to help us with the translation. Before we cross the Zambezi River, we pick up Manuel Chitui at his home in Matundo and take him along to Tete. The two men then go and see the Registrar. They return with the news that the church registration is still in the pipeline. There is nothing new to report. Marion and I check in at Piscina for one night as tomorrow we travel on to Mutarara. Joash is spending the night with Chitui. In the morning they show up in time to have breakfast with us in the outdoor restaurant here at Piscina.

Mutarara is a small town on the north banks of the Zambezi River not far from the southern tip of Malawi. We start out early and after traveling 90 kilometers east on the tarmac road that leads to Zobue, we turn south and drive another 220 kilometers on a bush road that has countless dips and bends in it. We come across trains that have been blown off their tracks. They now lie silent, resting on their sides. When we see a bombed-out trestle with the engine lying at the bottom, I stop to take some pictures. While climbing the bank for a closer look, Marion calls out for me to not go any further. Chitui had informed her that there might still be live land mines lying about! I return back to the vehicle making sure I step in my own tracks.

It is almost two o'clock when we arrive. The town has been devastated by wars, and the four-kilometer-long railway bridge that spans the Zambezi River linking Mutarara with Sena is out of commission. Two spans on this side collapsed when bombs planted by Renamo rebels exploded knocking the pillars from under it. United Nations is planning to repair the damage and convert the bridge for road traffic. They hope to have it done by the end of this year. It was the world's longest bridge when built in 1934. The first train crossed on its way to Malawi the following year. It includes a footpath and is truly a remarkable feat of engineering.

We hunt for a place that serves something to eat and find there is only one establishment in town. It is nothing to write home about! We sit around and wait for over an hour before food is served. It is chicken and rice. I book a room for us and one for Joash, Chitui, and Ezerone in the only place available in town. It was once a respectable hotel. Today it is vacated and in disrepair, except for a few rooms upstairs which contain beds and no other pieces of furniture. The rooms containing the toilet and showers are filthy! No running water. It needs to be brought in with a pail from a container outside. The whole bottom floor is infested with bats. Their stench is unbearable! Oh, well, this is Mozambique!

At dusk we hold a service in this sprawling town. It is in a lean-to that is attached to the leader's hut. This is a very poor place indeed! Fifty appear to hear my message and I pray for those who seek repentance. We finally return to our room. The door cannot be locked for the night as the lock is missing! There is a bent nail though that I can turn to keep the door closed. The alarm on the Nissan goes off at 11:30 P.M. I get up and see nothing from my window, but Marion spots someone running away carrying a torch (flashlight) from her side of the room. At midnight, a drunkard shouting and singing interrupts us a second time. He carries on for some time. In spite of these interruptions, we do get some sleep.

Marion and I do not shower this morning, as the showers are just too dirty. I do not take a shave either. We have tea and bread for breakfast. The men traveling with us are hungry and order eggs. It is a misty morning. Our service is at a different spot from last night. Again, fifty villagers show up for the Word of God and many of them want prayer afterwards. We take leave and commence our journey back to Tete. Midway to the tarmac road, we stop at Doa and hold a service with the villagers that have gathered on top of a hill. It is too steep for the vehicle to climb, so we ascend it on foot. There is a lot of singing before my message. Many respond to it and ask for prayer. Marion is presented with a live chicken which she will give to Chitui and his wife.

The Nissan develops a fuel problem while we are still on the bush road. It runs a short distance and then stops. We offer up a prayer for the Lord to help us. A vehicle stops soon afterwards and tries to assist us. We make it to the main road before it starts acting up again. It is dark by now. The diesel that I bought yesterday at Moatize must have been quite dirty. The rest of the way to Tete, about 85 kilometers, the vehicle stops numerous times. Each time, I get it to run again only after draining the fuel filter and bleeding the line. A dirty job and a knuckle scraper! It is 7 P.M. when we arrive at the motel. I am tired and grimy. The double room we had two days ago has been taken, so Marion and I end up in separate rooms. It has been a hectic day that we will long remember.

It was a quiet night for both Marion and me as our rooms are further away from where they drink and brawl. She said someone knocked on her door during the night, and when she looked out the window it was a young man. He left when Marion refused to open the door. I had no one come to my door. My hands look tough this morning. I have many blisters and scrapes on my fingers and knuckles from working on the fuel line last night.

After we finish our business with the leaders here, we locate a garage that offers to fix our vehicle. They remove the fuel tank and drain a lot of water and dirt from it. They also discover one of the valves in the fuel line clogged with dirt. Once cleaned out, the motor is again running normal. Praise the Lord!

We are told that the President of Mozambique, who came yesterday to Tete, is still in town but we do not see him. It is time for Marion and me to move on to Harare so that we can get there before dark. We put Joash on a bus for Malawi, bid farewell to Chitui, and depart for Harare.

*　　*　　*

I am returning to Mozambique after an absence of four months. On this trip, I am starting out from Blantyre where I have just spent five days with the church in Malawi. I have Joash with me. The road to the border is full of potholes and the numerous cyclists slow us down even more. We pass through tea plantations for most of the way. Reach the border at 10:30 A.M. It takes some time to fill in all the required papers on the Mozambican side. Two men from one of our churches are present and assist me in Portuguese, as the border officials are limited in the English language.

When we enter the town of Milange, I must report at the police station and then the district commissioner. They want to know why we are in the area. After a long time of waiting and moving from one office to another, I am free to go. We finally reach our destination, Katapwa Village, located eight kilometers from town. After all the greetings, we eat at the church leader's house. Then it is back to the mud-and-wattle church for a service. I teach and preach to those who have come from several congregations. Many accept Christ. I give out Bibles and Book One in the TEE program to the church leaders. They are in the Nyanja language.

We return to Milange and book in at the only guesthouse in town. Locals run it. Joash has his own room and so do I. It is ten feet square, not very big! The wooden bed has a three-inch mattress and a small portable fan is hanging from the ceiling. There is a very small corner sink right next to a shower. The water is cold but I take one anyway. I have a bite to eat in their kitchen before turning in. It is only 8:30 P.M., but there is nothing else to do. The Nissan is parked inside the compound not far from my room.

I sleep nine hours! The wooden shutters on the windows have kept out the light. I peer through a hole and notice that my vehicle fared okay. I hear termites above me in the reed mat that serves as a ceiling. There is only cold water in the tap and that quits running in the middle of my shave! No mirror on the wall so I use the one I have brought along. How fortunate of me that I did. It is so crowded in here that to get to the toilet seat I must squeeze by the sink and then step across the shower stall! Water is running into my room this morning. It is coming from under the wall that separates my room from Joash's. His sink must be leaking.

Today we travel to Tete by way of Blantyre. We reach our destination at 4 P.M. We pick up Chitui at his house and visit with him until dark. The Certificate of Registration for the church has not yet arrived from Maputo.

Joash, who came with me, is spending the night here at Piscina as well. It rains heavily during the night. There is also a lot of wind causing the power to go off and on.

After breakfast we leave for Mutarara. Not long after we get on the dirt road, it becomes very rough. There has been plenty of rain in this area since my last visit. Before we even get as far as Doa, we come across a lorry stuck in the middle of the road. The driver informs us that it is far worse down the road. Do we carry on? I am unable to squeeze by the lorry without also getting bogged down in the swamp. So I turn back after having covered only 50 kilometers since leaving the tarmac.

Along the way I have a flat tire when still on the dirt road. Put on the spare that already has seen its better days. Wash the vehicle when we reach the main road, as it is covered with mud. The men find some water from a well at a nearby village. From here, Chitui and Ezerone catch a ride back to Tete. Joash and I carry on to Malawi, reaching Blantyre without any further problem. The bald tire held out!

Six
Reaching Ever Further

I leave Marion at home and head out for Mozambique. It is time to go again and assist the church in their outreach. This time I pick up Moyo at Katete, and take him along to help me with the translation. It takes a little longer this time at the Mozambican border. There is no insurance agent for the vehicle here at Cassacatiza as there is at Zobue. Therefore, as on my last trip through here, I pay for it when I reach the bridge that spans the Zambezi River. Check in at Piscina. Moyo will sleep here as well. I was already sleeping when Joash from Malawi and Chitui show up. Talk to them for a while before returning to bed.

A frog disturbs me during the night. It has gotten into my room somehow. This morning I throw it out. Joash, Chitui, and two others arrive in time for breakfast. They and Moyo travel with me to Samoa Village. To get there I first must drive 100 kilometers on the road that leads to Zobue. Then I turn off left onto a bush track and bump along for another ten kilometers. Finally, we reach our destination. It is a village that is well hidden in the midst of trees. Is this one of those "ends of the earth" that my Master commissioned me to go to?

Around 100 villagers attend the service that is being held under a large shady tree. They either sit on the ground or on logs. After my message, it takes me some time to pray for all those who want help. Two of them who are oppressed by demons receive deliverance. Several women who are barren ask for prayer so that they can bear children. Marion should be here for that. She has prayed for many who then bore children. Often the husband is at fault and so I have them come forward and pray for them too. Before we leave I give out Bibles and literature, all in Nyanja. The women and youth receive material as well.

Our second service is at the turn off that leads to Doa and Mutarara. This is where we had stopped to wash the mud off the vehicle on my last trip. The men had witnessed to the villagers when they went to fetch water. The village is called Madama and a church has sprung up here since then! I share the Word and pray for those who want prayer. It is a friendly group. We drive back to Tete and eat our first meal since early morning. Chitui and his two friends return to their homes in Matundo, but Joash is staying with Moyo for the night.

This morning I am traveling to Mutarara, where I failed to get to four months ago because of the rains and bad roads. I am told it is better now. Chitui and two more of our Mozambican leaders are with me, besides Moyo and Joash. The muddy section on the dirt road has been repaired and we reach Doa without any problem. It is noon when we arrive at the church on top of the hill. I preach and then pray for those who come forward. We are served food before taking leave. It is difficult to find a latrine around here!

It is 2 P.M. when we leave for Mutarara. It's a hot day! Pass many bare-breasted women working in their fields or walking along the road. Many of the older ones are carrying loads on their heads. It's very backward out here!

The road keeps deteriorating more and more, the further I travel. (A good thing I turned back in January!) There are ruts, washouts, potholes, and puddles of water. Driving through one section, the muddy water rushes over the hood of the vehicle! It was that deep! At another spot, I come across a lorry stuck and I have to skirt around it through tall grass and water. I make it with the Lord's help.

We finally arrive in Mutarara at dark and book in at the same bat-infested hotel as last time. I find out today there are also rats in the place! It is 7:30 P.M. before the chicken and rice we ordered at the nearby restaurant is ready. After the meal, we retire for the night. It is warm and, oddly, no mosquitoes. I am tired tonight. Even the smell of bats, or knowing there are rats about, does not deter me from my getting some much-needed sleep.

The fleabites from yesterday are itchy this morning. Wake up at 4 A.M. and cannot go back to sleep. It is already hot and humid at this early hour in this war-torn town. I shave with water in my tumbler, as the sink is just too unclean. Drive the Nissan to a nearby dam and wash off the mud before taking my breakfast. We eat at the same place as last night. The restaurant was probably attractive in its heyday, but not anymore. It is now dilapidated and unsanitary.

Our service is here in town. On our way I notice that the bridge that spans the Zambezi River has been repaired. It is now open for traffic but not for trains for which it originally was built. After my message, all the adults come up for prayer. Have all sinned? Give out Bibles and literature. At noon I start out for Nsanje, Malawi. Joash and Moyo are coming with me but the Mozambican leaders are catching a lift back to Tete. It is 40 kilometers north to the border along a meandering road. There used to be quite a big post here on the Mozambican side but now all these magnificent buildings are in shambles. What war can do to a country!

The Customs and Immigration post for Malawi is several kilometers away from the Mozambican border. This is common in Malawi. I find this so at every border I have crossed thus far. There is a five-kilometer stretch of no-man's land between their Customs and Immigration office and the border. The officials are cordial as we check in. We travel twenty-five more kilometers and reach Nsanje at noon. I will be here in Malawi for a while visiting churches before resuming my trip back to Lusaka.

*   *   *

Time has come for me to return to Mozambique. But I am having trouble this morning finding diesel for my vehicle in Lusaka. And when I finally do, I have to wait in line at the pumps. Finally we are able to leave, albeit an hour later than planned. Moyo is accompanying me again. I enter Mozambique at Cassacatiza and reach Tete at dark. It took a little longer at the border today, plus some of the road was rough. We book in at Piscina, the motel managed by the Portuguese couple. Chitui and two others show up and we visit. Then, it is time to retire. It's been a long day. Put in 840 kilometers since leaving Lusaka.

Today our service is across the river at Matundo. But first there is a meal at Chitui's house. The church building sits in a hollow surrounded by huts and huge rocks. About seventy-five show up, half of them are children. The musical instruments they play during the singing are homemade. Besides drums, they shake empty cans containing pebbles. It is all quite loud! After the message,

I lead them in a communion service, their first here in this church. Just as we ended, a dust storm blows in. The sky gets dark and dust blows through the cracks in the walls. We say goodbye and reach the motel just as it starts to rain. It pours heavily for some time accompanied by strong winds.

Today Chitui and Moyo travel with me to the town of Chimoio, located 385 kilometers south of Tete. It is on the main road to Beira and we arrive at noon. Stop for a soft drink at the Moinho motel that is in the shape of a large windmill. Chitui leads us to a place on the outskirts of town where the leader of the church lives. Here his wife feeds us before the service. The people here do not understand Nyanja, only Shona or Portuguese. So Moyo translates my sermon into Nyanja, and then by Chitui into Portuguese. So I have two interpreters! It's not to my liking, as I have to wait longer than usual for my turn. Pray for all those who come forward. There are two young men who are oppressed by demons in their dreams. I bind the spirits and command them to leave and never return.

We leave at 4 P.M. and drive on to Beira, a good 200 kilometers west of here. It is a tarmac road and we make good time arriving two hours later. It is dark when we drive into the narrow yard at the church leader's house on the outer edge of the city. His name is Armando Baltazar. It is late before we eat. Then at ten o'clock we are given rooms to sleep in. There are plenty of mosquitoes around. I am glad for the net I brought along. Using my traveling mat and sleeping bag tonight as I'm bunked on the floor. I keep the shutters on the window open, as it is stifling hot in the room.

At midnight, I hear some shooting. Half an hour later a dog starts barking. I can see the Nissan through my open window. Nothing happens. In the morning I am told that it was the nearby police scaring away suspicious looking banditos. I need a bath this morning as I did a lot of sweating during the night. There is a service this morning in the church here. They gather in the small mud and wattle building and I again must use two interpreters for my sermon. We pray for all those who request our help.

Baltazar knows some Swahili that he picked up while working up in northern Mozambique along the Tanzania border. He is presently one of our national leaders. I visit with him some before driving out to look at the Indian Ocean. There are not many on the beach. If this were Mombasa, it would be crowded. Beira is the second largest city in Mozambique, Maputo being the largest.

There is nothing special for shopping here in the city, so I return to Baltazar's place for another service in the afternoon. We observe the Lord's Supper after the message. Also teach about customs that hinder the growth of a Christian. The women here do a lot of ululating and interrupting the speaker with a song. There are many who are sick, so I take time to pray for their healing. Give out some Bibles at the close of our meeting.

I am glad for the net, as there are a lot of mosquitoes tonight. It is quiet outside, except for a nearby disco. Up at five, pack my things and load the vehicle. Take a wash in the outdoor enclosure but do not shave. There are a lot of mosquitoes around at this early hour. After we eat, Chitui, Moyo, and I leave for Quelimane. The tarmac road ends at Dondo, just 30 kilometers west of Beira. Here I turn north onto a road that is passable only with 4x4 vehicles during the rainy season. It is now October and dry, so we should be okay. I carry on.

I first run into gravel, then long sandy patches, and finally potholes—some of them large enough to bury a vehicle! The road passes through forests and heavy undergrowth. There are blown up bridges along the way and to get to the other side, I must cross the dry riverbeds. Railway tracks run alongside the road with rusting train engines and their cars strewn about, blown off the tracks by land mines. There are many more remnants of their civil war along this road than the one between Tete and the Zambia border. There are experts along this stretch who are in the process of removing land mines. We come across their little red flags with the skull and crossbones on them that they use as markers.

After we pass Caia, we reach the Zambezi River. We sit around in the hot sun for quite a while before the small ferry arrives to take us across. The river is quite wide at this point. At one time there were plans to build a bridge to reach the other bank. Work had actually started, but today it is a forgotten dream.

The remaining 200 kilometers to Quelimane is a nightmare as well! It had tarmac at one time but is now in a mess. Again we find bridges blown out of commission, some of them very large and impressive! The remaining twenty or so kilometers to town are so badly corrugated and pockmarked that it is taking me forever to reach Quelimane. It is 7 P.M. and dark when we finally enter town, and I stop at the first hotel we see. The Pensao is roomy and mostly empty. It takes them over two hours to serve us a simple meal! When we finally turn in, it is 10 P.M. It has been a long and exhausting day, traveling over very rough roads, the longest stretch I have faced in Africa—all 400 kilometers of it!

I take time to shave this morning. No running water, so I wash myself with the water in the bucket. For a city hotel, they offer poor service. It takes an hour and a half for them to serve us breakfast! I find them very laid back here in Mozambique. After we check with the Registrar General about church registration here in Zambezia Province, I start out for Milange. I already have clocked 2,000 kilometers on this trip since leaving Lusaka. Today, I turn the Nissan homeward.

The road has some tarmac till we reach Mocuba, then it is sand and potholes. We eat at a restaurant in Mocuba. It takes them an hour and a half to serve the meal! While waiting, I chat with someone who knows Swahili. During the civil war in this area, he had spent eleven years in Kenya where Swahili is spoken widely. Along the bush road to Milange, we come across shelled out buildings that were once attractive shops and homes. But the war ruined them all. What a pity!

Arrive at Milange before dark and check in at the small guesthouse where I had spent a night several months ago. The little ceiling fan above the bed is still there. I get the same room—number seven. Lucky me! Chitui and Moyo each have a room as well. We eat our evening meal, discuss the work for a while, and then turn in. I am glad that the long stretch of bad roads is now behind me! The road from Beira to Milange via Quelimane has been very rough on the vehicle and on the driver. I would not like to drive it again anytime soon. It has been another hot day!

The bed has the same three-inch mattress. I can feel the boards beneath me. Still no mirror, so I use mine again. A good thing I saved some water last night for shaving, as there is no running water this morning. We are again served potato chips with our meal, even at breakfast! They actually taste good and the rice as well. Coconut oil is widely used in their cooking. I have noticed that prices have shot up in Mozambique. Fuel is up, and so is food. Soft drinks are over a dollar a bottle! Zambezia Province is really cut off from the rest of the country due to the lack of bridges across the Zambezi River. The people, especially here in Milange, depend entirely on Malawi for everything.

Before going to Chunguza Village for a service, I report my presence to the district commissioner. He is busy and it is after eleven before we get to see him. He is friendly and welcomes our assistance in his district. I am given freedom of movement. Finally, we are in church and I share the Word of God. Most of them want prayer, two of them for demonic oppression. There is a meeting afterwards with elections. Then, it is off to another church, about 18 kilometers further along the road. I have a flat on the way. After a short service we return to the guesthouse. The Christians gave me two live chickens, bananas, and rice as gifts this afternoon.

The night is again warm and I need only the thin sheet to cover me toward morning. The sweeper wakes me up at 3 A.M. while sweeping the courtyard in front of the rooms. Dust drifts through the shutters of my glassless window. I do not get much sleep after that and finally get up at six o'clock. After breakfast, I still give out some Bibles and literature to the church leader who shows up with my two hens that I left with him for the night.

I am going on to Malawi today, where I will be meeting with the national leaders in Blantyre before going on home. At the border, the Mozambican customs officer takes his time with us. He checks through the boxes that contain the Bibles and literature that are still left over for the work in Malawi. He also looks inside the water container, and even sniffs it! We resume our journey, when he has completed his investigation and finds no reason to keep us any longer. I am still traveling without a spare as there has been no place to repair it in Milange. I reach Blantyre safely and have it fixed. Finally! How many times is this now that I have been traveling on a wing and a prayer?

Seven
Near-Mishaps in the Bush

My trip to Mozambique today is through the border post at Cassacatiza, Moyo is traveling with me again so as to help me with the translation. Lost some time on both sides of the border because of waiting for the officers to show up from wherever they had wandered off to. It is after dark when we reach the bridge. Before crossing it, we check with Chitui whether he booked a couple of rooms for us at Piscina. He said that he did, but when we got there they were filled up. So we end up at the Zambezi Hotel, a place I have been to a couple of times. We eat our meal and then retire for the night. It is already 10 P.M. Hot and humid tonight.

I did not have to use a sheet, let alone a blanket. We are given tea and bread for our breakfast. Check at Piscina and discover they have a couple of empty rooms, so we move over there. The meals are better here than at the hotel. I pick up more of their local currency to use while here in Mozambique. Three of the national leaders—Chitui, Ezerone, and Francisco—show up and we talk about the progress of the work. I am told that today, February 14,1998, there now are 157 churches with 12,000 believers.

They inform me there was an earthquake recently not far from Morrumbala that has left many people homeless. A mountain split open killing at least 100 villagers, and many more are still missing. I will not be able to go there with relief aid this time as the quake and the rains have destroyed the road leading to the area. Instead, I will be going to Beira in the morning and from there fly to Maputo to meet the registrar general in the capitol about the church's registration. I have been invited by him personally to come there.

It has been another hot day! There is no cooling off during the night because the air conditioner in my room is not functioning properly. After a bite to eat, we leave Tete for Beira. Moyo, Chitui, and Francisco are traveling with me. When we reach Chimoio, I stop for a service. It is noon when the people arrive. I share the Word of God and then pray for those who need help. Give the church leaders tracts for his ministry before we leave.

A girl of about thirteen or fourteen comes up to me when we are saying goodbye and does something that no other African female has done before. She is following the Portuguese way of leave-taking by touching her cheek to mine, first on one side and then on the other. I am caught completely off guard! I learn later that some Africans in Mozambican cities do practice this custom taught them by their Portuguese employers.

We eat at Moinho, the place that looks like a huge windmill, before carrying on to Beira. The lowlands near Beira are flooded with fish camps standing in deep water. The altitude here in the swamps is only 100 feet above sea level! It is even lower when we reach the church on the outskirts of the city where Baltazar has his home. It is just 40 feet here. (At Tete it is 360 feet.) They have had water problems here, I am told. We check at the airport about tomorrow's flight but none are around. I will have to try the travel agent in the city tomorrow. After the evening meal, I retire in the vehicle for the night.

Spent a good night in the Nissan. It was better than outside with all the mosquitoes. I leave early for downtown to check on tickets for Maputo and learn that there is no room on today's flight. There is one tomorrow afternoon, but too late to find the offices still open and then for me to return. That would mean staying an extra day. The travel agent will not accept my credit card to pay for the tickets. I tried the Standard Bank and there, too, they refused to give me cash. I am told that all of Beira does not deal in credit cards as yet. So that means my trip to Maputo is off. I will have to try another route. We return to the home of Baltazar and take our breakfast of bread with tea. While we were in town, I stopped at the ocean to get a reading on my altimeter and it registered zero. So it is quite accurate.

Someone from Chemba Village appears with the news that he was sent by one of our pastors in Malawi to come and see the missionary. He says that his village wants me to plant a church in their area. We leave right after our meal of fish and rice. After traveling 95 kilometers on the main road towards Chimoio, I turn off and steer north onto a dirt road. I am told that Makimba Village we are going to is just a short distance away. After driving 10 kilometers, he directs me off the dirt road onto a footpath that leads through tall grass. By now we are not far from a National Park. The village is just ahead, I am told.

But after another five kilometers he tells me that it is just beyond the tall trees. We are now heading into a forest. Now behind which tree is it? We cross a swampy section that has water standing in deep holes. I am kept busy dodging them plus termite mounds that pop up out of nowhere! The tall reeds keep me from seeing far enough ahead. The radiator is getting filled up with grass seeds. Finally, we reach the village. It just appears out of nowhere! It is 22 kilometers from the tarmac road. Did he say that it was just a short distance away?

The villagers have already gathered when we arrive. It will soon be dark so we need to start the service immediately. They have erected a shelter for this occasion. It has a grass roof but no walls. They have brought several folding chairs for us to sit on. The men are seated on logs while the women and children are parked on the ground. I preach on "Where Are You?" (Genesis 3:8-13). Many respond to the message and kneel for prayer. Just as I finish my prayer and look up, I see some of those who had been kneeling jump up as a snake comes crawling out from among them! It slithers toward us and passes between the church leaders and me. Before I can take another breath the black mamba has vanished into the tall grass. A miracle no one got bitten!

Two girls said they felt something touch their legs while I was still praying. Thank you, Lord, for watching over all of us! I remind them of what I had just preached about, the devil coming into our midst to tempt us as he did with Adam and Eve. So the snake coming along was a good illustration to what I had been sharing in my sermon. With the Lord's protection, no one was hurt. No mishap. Not so with Adam and Eve. Was the Lord behind this little episode tonight?

After the service, we prepare for the night. It is pitch dark already. Heavy clouds have rolled in and, so, there is no moon. There is a fine mist coming down as I climb up onto the roof rack. I untie the traveling mat, sleeping bag, my luggage, and the things that belong to those who have come with me. After handing down all these items to Moyo, I turn around to dismount backwards.

As I step on the spare tire that is mounted on the rear door, my foot slips on the wet surface and I drop down onto my back with a thud! I remember my head hitting the hard ground and then all went black, for how long I do not know. The first thing I remember is Moyo trying to pull me up by the hand. I tell him not to bother. My head needs to clear first and then find out if anything is broken. I slowly get up under my own steam. Nothing appears to be broken, but I feel like my wind has been knocked out of me.

I am moving about when it comes time to eat the food that the women have prepared for their guests. Before I can call it a day, I need to take a shower, as I am filthy from the fall I just had. The back of my white shirt is black from landing on the ground. When I get inside the enclosure to take a shower, I have trouble washing my back. My muscles are getting stiff and it is difficult drying myself with the towel. Finally, I make my way to the vehicle and spread out my sleeping bag on the back seats. I crawl inside and thank the Lord for keeping me from a more serious mishap. And now, Lord, grant me some sleep. It has been an extra full day.

I am spending a poor night in the vehicle, as my back is sore from the fall. A good thing there was no rubble or stones lying about where I fell. That really would have wrecked my back. How then would I have been able to get out of this place that is tucked away in the heart of the Mozambican bush? Surely the Lord is watching over me. I am unable to get comfortable in the back seat until toward morning. The rest are all sleeping outside on the ground. The mosquitoes are plentiful out there. One even got inside the vehicle. Up before dawn and take a wash.

There are no latrines around here. The villagers all use the maize fields. You are given a hoe to use when nature calls.

Drops of rain start falling before light this morning. I rebuke it in the name of the Lord! I pray that it will not rain, as that will make the roads even worse than what they already are. Even though it looks like it may rain any minute, it holds off. The Lord has heard my prayer! We leave the village at 6 A.M. and make our way back to the main road. Before we reach it, I stop and we wash the vehicle near a stream. It really needs it.

I stop at Nhamatanda and Baltazar drops off to return to Beira. I carry on to Tete. Chitui and Moyo are with me. It rains off and on along the way. I must stop a couple of times to stretch my back muscles. My neck is sore and stiff as well. We reach Tete safely. It is very hot here along the Zambezi River, at least 100 or more degrees Fahrenheit! I book Moyo and myself in at Piscina. After our noonday meal, I rest some. It is good to lie flat on my back after the long drive. My shoulder and chest muscles are sore and stiff. The men pray for me this evening.

I get up at 5 A.M. and take Moyo to the bus station. He leaves for Zambia in an hour. I have to work the stiffness out of my shoulders this morning. The lower part of my back is better but the top half is sore and stiff. It takes a while before I am limber enough to move freely. It feels as if I got whiplash from the fall. Involuntarily, I must have held my head up and the sudden jar strained the muscles. I leave at 7:30 A.M. for Blantyre, Malawi. Chitui is traveling with me and will carry on to Milange from there. It is closer for him this way through Malawi instead of around Mutarara where it is all bush roads.

*　　*　　*

Three months later I am on my way to Mozambique. This time I am flying to Maputo concerning the registration of the church. Go by road to Victoria Falls and then fly from there to Harare. There I catch the flight to Maputo and arrive in the afternoon. Take a taxi to the Assemblies of God guesthouse. A German/Portuguese married to an American woman operates it. Their names are Hans and Evangeline Casquerio. I meet an Angolan who is staying here and we talk. It is helpful, as I want to go there soon. Turn in for the night at ten o'clock.

It is cool during the night. In morning there is a haze due to the grass fires. I saw them from the plane yesterday as we were nearing the airport. At nine, I take a taxi to the office of the Minister of Religious Affairs and find Chitui there as we had arranged. When we are finally able to see him, he tells us to return tomorrow. Chitui thinks this is a sign he wants us to hand him some money. Should we do it tomorrow?

Before we return to the guesthouse, I cash some U.S. dollars that I have brought with me. The rate is 11,900 Meticais to a dollar! Their currency is steadily devaluating. I book Chitui into the guesthouse here. I must communicate with Chitui in Nyanja, as he still does not speak English. He tells me there are now 180 churches. The Frank Neuenburgs, a couple that Marion and I met while in Uganda are now residing here in Maputo. We visit a while. He remembers Marion's stories of our guardian angels.

I still get a pain in the right side of my chest when I lie on my back for some time. To get rid of it, I have to turn on my right side. The accident happened on February 16, 1998. That's three months ago. At 9 A.M., Chitui and I are back at the minister's office. Today, he is in a very accommodating mood. The process has begun; we are to return in the afternoon. We do. Papers are then signed and pictures taken as I have along my camera. By the way, I give the minister his gift, after he has helped us! Chitui is the one who hands it to him. Frank takes me for a drive in the evening to show me the Indian Ocean and a few other sites. I finish all my business with Chitui tonight, as tomorrow he returns by bus to Tete.

I am up early as the flight leaves at 7:30 A.M. for Harare. A taxi takes me to the airport, as well as the Angolan. He will be flying on to Luanda, Angola. The plane makes a stop at Beira before reaching Harare where I am spending the night. The plane to Victoria Falls does not fly until tomorrow morning. As arranged, Guni shows up and we discuss the work here in Zimbabwe. I call Marion tonight and she reports that all is fine. She plans to pick me up at the airport when I land at Victoria Falls.

*   *   *

On my next trip, Oscar Ndao is traveling with me. When we arrive at the border, we find the Zambian customs officer not present. It is 4:30 P.M. before he shows up. This will take us into Tete well after dark. On the Mozambican side the delay was less, even though the officer had to be fetched from the nearby beer party in the village. The road becomes quite rough by the time we get to Tete, which is 7:30 P.M. We find Chitui still waiting for us at the bridge. He comes with us to Piscina. We talk and after supper he walks home. I turn in tired from navigating the vehicle over 800 kilometers around and through all the potholes.

I rested well during the night. After breakfast, Oscar and I go to town where I buy a razor as I forgot mine at home. Also, pick up some local money. The rate is now

12,700 Meticais per U.S. dollar! Chitui makes his appearance and we discuss the work. It is growing and there is a need for bikes for five different district overseers. In the afternoon Oscar preaches to fifty people in the service at Matundo. Then we pray for those who want spiritual strength and physical healing. We are invited to stay for supper. While waiting for the food to be prepared, we witness a fight between a Portuguese young man and a Mozambican. The latter is quite drunk and so the former has no problem getting the best of him. Chitui writes his TEE test. We return to the hostel after our meal of *nsima* and meat.

We leave after breakfast for Samoa Village, picking up Chitui and Francisco along the way. The bush road is muddy and filled with holes. There are 185 who have gathered in the shade of large trees for the service. I am told that others failed to come because of the nearby fast-flowing river. There is lots of singing. The drums are very loud and give me a headache! Finally, it is time for me to preach the Word. Oscar translates. Many respond and it takes a long time to get through the line. Two are oppressed with demons that appear in dreams at night and they see lights flashing in their rooms! I pray the prayer of deliverance over them. After we are done, we return to Tete.

It is Valentine's Day and I am able to get through to Livingstone on the phone here at Piscina. I surprise Marion as I had intended to do. She says that the roses I had ordered for delivery on Valentine's Day have arrived. A complete surprise as well! She too has been at a service in the village. So we both were out in the bush on Valentine's Day preaching the gospel in separate countries 1,300 kilometers apart!

I have a tough night. The air conditioner quits running so there is no air circulating. The mosquitoes are now free to move about. I manage to kill one of them, but already I have been bitten a couple of times. To keep them at bay, I leave the lights on from midnight and sleep some the rest of the night. Chitui and two others show up after breakfast and we discuss the work. We also go to town for a few things. I mail Tiffany a postcard. She collects them and wants me to send her one from each country I visit. In the afternoon, we again have a service at Matundo. I preach this time and we pray for those seeking help. I am moved to another room tonight where the air conditioner works. No trouble with mosquitoes tonight.

Up early as Oscar and I are returning to Zambia today. Chitui shows up before we leave and has breakfast with us. We have a safe trip to the border. Pass through it without an incident.

*   *   *

I am entering Mozambique, this time from Malawi. I have just visited the work there and now will do the same here. Paffett Chomanika is with me, and so is Chitui. He came yesterday from Tete and met up with me in Blantyre as prearranged. The border posts at Mulanje, Malawi and Milange, Mozambique are just across from each other. This is the only place I have been where the Malawian border post is not five kilometers away from the border! I cross both sides without a problem. To get local currency, I cash money with the Mozambican official.

We check in at the guesthouse that I usually go to and find that it has improved greatly! A restaurant, plus more rooms, has been built across the road from it. I am given a room in this new section. A real shocker! We have our meal and then talk with the district overseer and

Chitui about the work in this district. It rains heavily while we sit and chat. I can see the mountain where one year ago a spring erupted near the top and water gushed down carrying away people and houses. Many died. The path the water took can still be seen. It is visible from the hostel. It is still raining when I retire for the night. I discover a card and some sweets in my luggage. Marion put them there before I left. She does these things often, very thoughtful of her.

I sleep quite well. No mosquitoes. Did not even use the sheet, as it is very humid here in Milange. There is a screen on the window and I leave it open. The water goes off at six this morning, so I end up using my bottled water for shaving. Fortunately, I had a splash bath with the water they had in the bucket before it quit. After breakfast, I drive out to a village that is 20 kilometers into the bush. It is hot and humid inside the church. There are over two hundred present for the service. Chomanika translates the message into Nyanja for me. Many come forward for repentance and some for healing. This takes some time.

After the service I teach the pastors and church leaders on doctrinal issues and the ordinances. There are now 238 churches in Mozambique! There is a pastor who got burned by a lightning bolt when it struck a tree near him. The whole front of his body is burned from his face to his feet. Of course, there are those who are saying that he had been bewitched! I carried on teaching until the food is ready to be served. It is now mid afternoon. They are slow here with their meals, even at the hostel where we are staying. I am given a stock of bananas, when we take leave for Milange.

It is raining this evening. I kill a big cockroach in my room. I have noticed there are no spiders here! The houses in Lusaka and Livingstone are full of them. We are forever killing these eight-legged creatures but they keep multiplying just the same. There are many geckoes here. Maybe that is why. They catch spiders for their meals. The night is hot and humid. After breakfast, I start my journey back to Malawi and then on to Lusaka and finally Livingstone. Chomanika and Chitui come with me as far as Blantyre.

Eight
Traveling Hardships

It is 7 A.M. before Marion and I can start our journey for Mozambique. Pray with the workers as we always do before saying goodbye. The Great East Road is okay as far as the bridge that spans the Luangwa River. Then the patchwork begins. Between Petauke and Katete it is really bad with potholes that take up the whole road. No dodging them! At noon, we stop under a tree and eat the lunch that Marion made for the road. I fuel up at the filling station in Katete and then head for Mozambique. We experience no problem at the border. They are fixing the road as we near Tete, so there are a lot of detours. It is 4:30 P.M. when we reach our destination. It took us nine and a half hours to cover the 820 kilometers from Lusaka. Marion took it quite well.

We book in at Tete Motel, a new lodging place alongside the Zambezi River on the east side of town. Asians are managing it. It is a cleaner place than Piscina. Still new! We eat supper in the dining room. No one else around but us! We have the whole place to ourselves. There is a TV in our room but it has only one channel, and it is in Portuguese. By nightfall, Chitui has not shown up as he usually does. Chomanika was to have met us here today as well. I had sent both of them telegrams of our arrival dates.

We have a good night of rest. Check out after breakfast and pick up the insurance for the vehicle, as they did not have any at the border. We then check on Chitui at his house and find him at home. No, he did not receive the telegram I sent three weeks ago. We unload most of the tracts we brought along, plus the Certificates for Baptism and Child Dedication. We communicate with him in Nyanja. Next, we go to the post office and call the school in Malawi where Chomanika teaches. We are told that he is not there. He may not have received my telegram either! We wait for him all day and when he does not show up, we check back into the motel for the night.

We are going to Mutarara for sure today so we check out and leave after breakfast. It is 300 kilometers to Mutarara. The dirt road turns worse and worse the closer we get to Doa. There are many washouts and ruts along the way. One of the back tires blows when a sharp rock pierces it! We drive the rest of the way without a spare. We cannot stop for a service at Doa as planned, as I am trying to get to Mutarara before we have another puncture. We finally make it by mid afternoon.

There are no tires or tubes available in town. Someone who has a workshop sells me an old tire that already is bald. It is twelve-ply, so it should do if we need it. The tube is fixed with a cold patch. Hopefully, it will hold when carrying a load. Marion and I book in at a small guesthouse that opened since our last visit. The hotel we stayed at previously has deteriorated even more. The bats are still there as well! The guesthouse is nothing more than a row of small rooms attached to each other with a shower and a latrine at the far end. Chitui and his wife, who came along this time, are staying here for the night as well.

We discover there is an eating-place right next to the

Zambezi River. A couple that are part Portuguese run it. He has lived here all his life. (Their son operates the workshop we were at earlier.) Their food is the best we have eaten since coming to Mutarara. Marion and I turn in at 9 P.M. The rooms are only about ten feet square, and the beds are narrow. We are using our sleeping bags that we brought along, as the bedding looks like they may have fleas. There is no hot water in the bathroom, only cold water that they carry in with a bucket from the river. The concrete toilet bowl is flushed with water from the same bucket. There is nothing sanitary around here!

It rains heavily during the night. There is no water this morning, unless you order it. Marion and I wash our faces with the water that we have brought with us. Hopefully, we will get to a place tonight where we will be able to shower properly. We eat at the same place as last night. Chitui has found someone who knows English and can translate for us. His name is Domingo. He learned to speak English while in Malawi where he fled to during the war.

Our service this forenoon is held in a building that lacks a roof. They quickly stick up a sheet of plastic above the section where we are to sit. Forty-five people show up for the service. Many come for prayer after my message that Domingo translated for me. After the service we drive across the bridge to Sena. It is our first time to cross the four-kilometer span. It is narrow and was built for trains alone. The tracks are still there. But now it is for vehicles only. Because it is so narrow, vehicles cross in one direction every fifteen minutes. Guards at the barriers keep time.

At Sena we purchase sacks of maize for the widows and the needy. Also, buy a bicycle for the district overseer. A truck is hired to haul the people and the things we bought for them back across the river to Mutarara. Then Chitui, Domingo, and we carry on towards Caia. Along the way we stop for a while to eat our lunch that Marion had prepared. At Caia I turn in to show Marion the ferry that carried me across the Zambezi River on my previous safari in this area. The river is very full, washing away the banks even more.

We leave the river behind and drive on toward Beira with intentions to stop at Inhamitanga for the night. I do not want to travel after dark on this remote road. But we do not notice the sign in the dim light and miss the small town. When we realize the mistake, instead of turning back, we drive on to the next town called Inhaminga. It is now 6:30 P.M., well after dark. We ask someone where we could find a guesthouse for the night and were directed to one run by the Roman Catholics. We are served supper two hours later. There is no electricity in the dormitory. We are given candles and a worker brings in hot water so that we can wash up before retiring for the night. The bedding looks clean, so we do not have to use our sleeping bags. We thank the Lord for bringing us through another day.

Marion and I had a good rest. It rained during the night. Only cold water this morning, so we make do. After breakfast in their restaurant, we leave Inhaminga behind us at 8:30 A.M. for Beira. We still have at least 285 kilometers left to travel before reaching our destination. The road is rough and runs through a forest. It's a rockin' and rollin' through countless deep mudholes and washouts along the way. We pass railroad cars lying on their sides and machines of war forsaken and rusting beside the road, all relics of the civil war destroyed by land mines. Not much traffic on this lonely road, only a few lorries and a bus with a goat perched on top of the luggage rack that is calmly trying to keep its balance.

Finally, at one o'clock we reach the tarmac highway at Dondo! It is a relief to get onto a good road again. When we reach the outskirts of Beira, we turn in at Baltazar's place. The children are in the process of making sweets out of shredded coconut and brown sugar. It tastes yummy! Marion buys the whole lot. There are palm trees on his lot that right now are loaded with ripe coconuts. Baltazar has someone here that can shimmy up the trunk and knock them down. Amazing! (On my last visit, he had sent several back with me for Marion.)

Marion and I book into a hotel in town, while Chitui and Domingo are staying with Baltazar for the night. We do not eat in the restaurant but snack on the things from Marion's basket. It is very windy tonight. We have traveled 1,500 kilometers thus far since leaving Lusaka.

The wind is still blowing this morning, wiping up dust along the streets. From our window we see huge waves with white caps rolling in from the ocean onto the empty beaches. After breakfast we move over to another hotel as this one is not that great and does not have an enclosed parking lot. Our Nissan had to spend the night out on the street. We also go hunting for a set of new tires and tubes. When we find them we have them installed. The Lord has again looked after us during our time of limping along on a crutch until we can walk properly!

I take Marion to the beach and show her the Indian Ocean. It is too windy to stroll along its sandy shore, but we take time to visit the site where years ago the *Macuta* foundered after running ashore when the tide went out. Its rusty hulk is there as a reminder of its mishap. We eat at a restaurant on the beach.

By 2 P.M. we are at Munyava for a service. It is a new

church opened recently by Baltazar. It is situated in a poor section of the city. Houses are built right next to each other, barely leaving enough space between them to squeeze by. The eighty-plus are meeting outside as their mud building has collapsed. They are a robust bunch and are very happy to see us. The youth do a lot of dancing and stamping their feet.

It is our first time to see worshippers use short pieces of flat boards as instruments. They clap them together rather vigorously. It is very deafening! They also clap their hands together loudly. I preach and then pray for the many who seek help from the Lord. Afterwards they escort us to the vehicle, singing all the way unperturbed by all the attention they are creating!

Marion and I return to the hotel for our evening meal. We both are tired tonight. We have been giving out ever since leaving Lusaka. Our passion for Africa keeps us charged and ready to carry on with the commission of spreading the good news.

It is Mother's Day! We leave the hotel at 8 A.M. and drive over to Baltazar's place. We pick him up along with Chitui and Domingo and commence our journey to Chimoio. On the way we stop at Mafumbissa for a service. There are over 100 present to see us and hear us. There is plenty of singing by various choirs. While preaching, I have to stop the women who are ululating during my message. I tell them that I prefer them saying amen instead. Many come forward and it takes some time before Marion and I are done praying for them all. The women here do not touch cheeks with Marion when greeting her as they did yesterday at Munyava. The girls kiss my hand when I greet them. I think it should be the other way around.

After the service, we are told that two churches across the Pungoe River were flooded out during the rains. The people have lost their houses and crops! We take time and purchase twenty-one bags of maize at the market for the suffering families. Marion also gives them clothing that she brought along for this purpose. The district overseer receives a bicycle to assist him in his work. The women give us food to eat before we leave.

At Nhamatanda, Christians are waiting beside the road to greet us. There are some present that have walked all the way from the village where I fell off the Nissan and suffered whiplash. Bless their hearts! We are then asked to attend a service at a new church in Nhamatanda. Marion preaches as I am too drained. Afterwards we pray for them and carry on with our journey. We reach Chimoio at 5 P.M. and check in at Moinho Motel. After supper we still drive out to the church for a short service. It is already dark.

The wake-up call for prayer by Muslims is fifteen minutes late here in Chimoio. At Beira they were punctual at five o'clock each morning. We have tea and some of our cookies for breakfast. Then at eight o'clock, we drive to the church for a service where about fifty-five have gathered. They are a noisy lot here as well. The clapping by the men is about the loudest I have ever heard! It's enough to give me a headache. I preach and the Lord anoints the message. When the altar call is given, they all come for prayer.

Before we can leave for Tete, we buy maize for three widows and a bicycle for the district overseer. Then Baltazar catches the bus back to Beira, while Chitui and Domingo travel with us. We reach Tete mid afternoon and check in at Piscina, as the other motel is full. We are using our sleeping bags on top of the beds again as we did last night at Chimoio. I usually pick up fleabites here at Piscina, so this may help. Discuss finances with Chitui tonight and I give him money for a bicycle and for the church that is being built across the river at Matundo. Domingo returns to Mutarara tomorrow by any means possible.

Up at six this morning and discover a frog in my shoe when I stick in my foot! That gave me a start. We load our vehicle after breakfast and start our journey toward home. No problem along the way. Pass through the border without a hitch. Before we reach Lusaka, Marion spells me off behind the wheel when I get drowsy. This will have been a 4,000-kilometer trip when we finally arrive back home in Livingstone.

*   *   *

Paffett Chomanika is traveling with me on this trip to Mozambique. I have just completed my stay with the church here in Malawi and now it is time to visit the work in Mozambique. We start out from Nsanje, where Chomanika makes his home, and travel south to the border. It is an easy passage on both sides today. I change some dollars into Meticais with the moneychangers who are just young fellows. There is no bank here at Villa Nova, the Mozambican border post.

It is near noon when we reach Mutarara. After a short visit with the pastor, we eat at Piscina Restaurant. It is run by the part-Portuguese couple. It takes quite a while this time before the fish and rice reach our table. We book in at the same inexpensive place as I did last time when Marion was along. Chitui arrives, and so does Baltazar, in time for the service. I preach and as usual many request prayer for their needs. During our supper, the four of us talk about the work here in Mozambique. It is 10 P.M. when we turn in.

A couple of mosquitoes show up in my room during

the night. Use the insect spray I brought along to get rid of them. (Either breathe that or contract malaria!) I do not use a sheet to cover myself. Too hot! Take a splash bath this morning in the outdoor shower. I do not remove my shoes, as the concrete floor is not clean. Shave at the vehicle using the sideview mirror and my bottled water. We eat breakfast at the same restaurant that is beside the river and again have our share of soft drinks.

On our way to Morrumbala for a service, there is a sharp bang that appears to come from in front of the vehicle. Was it from a stone? When we reach the Shire River, we stop to wait for the ferry to pull in from the other side. I raise the hood of the Nissan to take a look at the engine and find to my surprise the battery has literally exploded! That is what the loud noise was about back down the road. What caused it? Heat? It is extremely hot today. The cover is wrecked, broken into several pieces and acid is splattered all over the engine and under the hood. I cannot go any further into unfamiliar territory with a damaged battery! I regrettably turn back to Mutarara. There is no battery, old or new, to be found anywhere in this backward town. Unbelievable! There is nothing else to do but to tie some plastic around the damaged battery so as to keep the acid from leaking and spreading.

We eat at Piscina Restaurant before beginning our return trip to Tete where I hope to find a new battery. Along the way, I stop at Salima Village where they are building a church out of burned bricks. I assist them with some money. The choir of young people sings for us. One of the fellows plays an instrument that he invented himself from bicycle parts! It is the first time for me to see one like this. He is quite an originator.

At Doa, we look for a place to spend the night but find nothing. Buy some supplies at a shop and then continue on to Jeke Village a short distance from Doa. There is a church here and they cook a meal for us. By now it is 9 P.M. Chomanika still preaches a message under a tree before everyone calls it a day. I take a wash in an outdoor enclosure before crawling into the Nissan for the night. There are some mosquitoes around.

In spite of mosquitoes, I keep the windows down an inch or so for air. I sleep well and wake up without any aches from sleeping on the front seats. There was plenty of room to move around. The sun is up at 4:30 A.M. and the women are already moving about. I manage to dress before anyone shows up at the vehicle. Shave and wash up in the outdoor enclosure made from reeds. The latrine is in bad shape with the grass around it not giving much of a covering. There is warm tea and buns for breakfast. Children are active this morning, even after running around late into the night.

In the service, I preach and God anoints the message. Many repent, and I also pray for the sick. I give them some money for the church they are building. At ten o'clock, we leave for Tete. The battery is holding out okay. Before we reach the tarmac road, I have a flat on the front tire. It seems with every trip on this stretch of rock-strewn road, I pick up a puncture or have a blowout! We reach town at 1:30 P.M. and I check in at Tete Motel. After lunch, I take the flat tire and have it repaired. They find a screw inside. It must have dropped from the back of a passing lorry. Purchase a battery and pick up the insurance for the vehicle, as they did not have it at the border. It is late before I get to bed.

The electricity goes off at six this morning so I take my shower in the dark. It is still off when I leave for the service at 8:30 A.M. There are eighty present in the church at Matundo. The building is not completed. Chomanika translates again and many come forward for help. There is a woman who is demon-possessed. The demon reacts when I am praying for the group. I deal with her and discover there are several of them tormenting her, even in her dreams. They are driven out in the name of Jesus. One of them lingers longer than the rest.

Chomanika catches a bus in the afternoon back to Blantyre. I return to the motel and spend the evening trying to refresh my memory the words I learned when Marion and I took Nyanja after moving to Zambia. I would still like to preach in it before leaving Zambia, the Lord willing. It is difficult to use Nyanja everywhere I travel in Zambia because of other languages that the tribes still adhere to in different provinces. I am unable to continually use Nyanja, as I was able to do with Swahili in Tanzania. Oh the endless languages and dialects I come across in almost every village here in Southern Africa!

Before finally dropping off to sleep, I unburden myself to the Lord. Where are the laborers who should be out here assisting me? The workload is increasing. I am thankful for those who are holding up my hands, but I need those who are also willing to go into battle, to fight the devil and drive him back! Where are they?

I wake up at 2:30 A.M. and do not go back to sleep. I am wide-awake. The work keeps running through my mind. The load is just too great. It is only with the Lord's help that I am able to carry on. Marion has often said, "Why are you doing all this?" It is for the Lord, of course. But for how long can I carry on like this?

At five o'clock, I get up and prepare for my return trip to Lusaka. All goes well and I reach the border in good time as they have just resurfaced the road. When I reach Lusaka, I call Marion at Livingstone. She informs me that all is well. Thank you, Lord, for watching over her!

Nine
The Zambezi River Floods

I wake up this morning at Grace Bandawe Center in Blantyre with fleabites on my body that itch something fierce. I just cannot make a trip to Malawi or Mozambique without getting attacked by them! It is because of sleeping in these cheap guesthouses. Chomanika and I leave for Tete at eleven o'clock. We make it through the border quite okay. There is lots of traffic nowadays at this crossing point. It rains along the way and even Tete is overcast when we arrive. The Zambezi River basin in Mozambique has been receiving very much rain recently and there has been flooding, especially from Mutarara to the Indian Ocean.

The road to Mutarara is impassable or else I would go there this trip. It will now have to wait until the next one when the rains are over and the roads have dried out. Reports have been that many homes are being swept away as they were further south during the floods a year ago. Many nameless people are without any possessions! A few are receiving aid but so many are unable to be in the right place at the right time. Is this to be their allotment in life, always reaching but never receiving their portion in life?

This happens in times of drought as well. Mothers begging for food while their naked children crowd around them. Old women are reduced to just skin stretched over feeble bones. Victims of famine struggle to survive, yet succumb to the inevitable. Death is never really welcome and yet it comes. How often we have witnessed these scenes during our years in Mbugwe, Tanzania! (*To a Land He Showed Us*, chapter eight)

Chitui is waiting for us when we arrive. He received both of my telegrams this time, the last one only yesterday. Most of the church leaders have come in for the business meeting. We go right into it and several new national leaders are elected. It is 8:30 P.M. when it ends. Chomanika and I are booked in at Piscina for the night. No hot water. I was looking forward to a hot bath, as it has been a humid afternoon in spite of it being overcast.

I have picked up more fleabites during the night! At nine o'clock in the morning we find ourselves in church at Matundo. There is singing before I bring the message. There is good attention and quite a few come forward for prayer. Evil spirits in dreams oppresses one of them. He, himself, had been a witchdoctor at one time and now the powers of darkness want him to return to his old profession. I pray for his deliverance. There are several who are sick and need the Lord to heal them. Finally, I pray for the new church leaders who have been elected to their national, provincial, and district posts.

Before we can call it a day, I teach for a couple of hours on some doctrinal issues and church administration. It was well worth the time, as they had many questions. In the end, I give out Bibles and ministerial booklets. It is late when Chomanika and I make our way back to Piscina. The leaders have been sleeping in the church while the local women cook for them. I climb into bed early as tomorrow I travel back to Zambia.

After taking Chomanika to the bus station at 5:30

A.M., where he will catch a bus to Malawi, I leave Tete behind me. It rains off and on as I travel. For my breakfast, I eat from the lunch box as I still have a few things left that the girls prepared for me when I took off from Lusaka. I am delayed at the border on the Zambian side. The immigration officer is taking his time scrutinizing my passport. When I tell him I am a missionary, he returns it to me. I guess he was suspicious of the many visas and rubber stamps I have in it from all the different countries I have been. I encounter more rain en route to Lusaka. I give Marion a call when I arrive at Avondale, my home away from home, and we talk a while.

* * *

Don Riley, the Regional Director for Africa, is traveling with me on this trip to see a portion of the work here in Southern Africa. The safari started in Zambia, then on to Malawi, and now we are on our way to Mozambique. We are starting out from Nsanje where we just spent a night in a small hostel. I replace the spare that got wrecked yesterday with the extra tire and tube I brought along. Thank the Lord that I did. The road has really deteriorated because of the heavy rains. It takes us an hour to reach the border. We pass through both border posts without a problem. I am unable to get enough local currency from the moneychangers; hopefully we will get some at Mutarara.

I am anxious to see how much destruction the floods have caused in this section of the Zambezi River. The news is that many homes, crops, and even lives have been swept away by the raging waters. Much aid will be required to assist the victims of this catastrophe of unimaginable proportion! Helicopters have been plucking individuals from rooftops and treetops where they have clambered to be rescued! Why, oh, why all this suffering here in Mozambique? Have they not had enough?

We pass several camps containing thousands of tents donated by World Vision for the flood victims! Medicine Without Borders and the Red Cross are assisting as well. I have never before in my life seen so many tents! Besides the boreholes, there are open tents serving as kitchens, and smaller ones for latrines, to accommodate the mass of refugees that have fled the flooded areas. To feed them there are countless bags of mealie meal stacked underneath roofs and in large storage sheds. What a change has taken place to the countryside since my last trip! Unbelievable!

When we reach Mutarara, we find Chitui waiting for us. A large refugee camp has been erected here as well. White tents as far as the eye can see! The Zambezi River has risen above its banks and people are paddling boats as a means of travel to ferry passengers across the flooded plain that was not there before. The water has washed away the road that leads to Morrumbala. It is incredible how the scenery has changed! It was on that road where my battery exploded. Water reaches the bat-infested hotel that we used to sleep in when we first came here. The river flooded the Piscina Restaurant that sits next to the river. Today we book in again at the shabby guesthouse that we had last time.

The bearing in the left front wheel is making a squealing noise, so I take the Nissan to the shop run by the part-Portuguese's son. He removes the wheel, tightens the bearing, and adds grease before replacing the wheel. It seems to work okay now. We eat our lunch at his parent's restaurant while he is working on the vehicle.

We can see the watermark on the wall where the river had risen to during the flood.

Our first service is at a small church tucked away among some large rocks. It is very hot inside the building and outside as well. The next service is at dark in the refugee camp. Many people show up to sing and then to hear Don preach. There is no moon and it is pitch black by now. Many accept the Lord. A woman starts crying while I am praying for her, and an ancestral spirit reacts in her violently. The demon's name is Oro. She also has a traditional spirit and a lion demon. It takes only five minutes to drive all three out in the name of Jesus Christ. Praise the Lord!

I am able to change some dollars into Meticais after the service. We eat at the grubby restaurant that is next to the guesthouse. I have not eaten any greens or fruit for the last three days, and there is none to be found here either. The lights in my room do not work tonight, so I do without. We all take a cold splash bath from a bucket. It helps to cool us off, as it was very hot all afternoon.

Five pastors have moved into the refugee camp along with their congregations and will stay there until the water subsides. They are given the basic mealie meal but have to search for their extra rations. So I assist them this morning with money for food supplements. I have picked up several fleabites since coming here. They are very itchy! What all a person has to endure for the gospel's sake.

I leave without breakfast. I think I am packed up enough. At the bridge, we have to wait until we are given the go-ahead by the guard. Cross the Zambezi River and take the road to Caia. The wheel bearing begins to squeal again! Do we carry on? We are a long way from any garage or service station. We decide to keep driving. The squeal keeps getting louder. We stop and have prayer, with Chomanika leading it. Without the Lord's help, we will not make it to Beira. The road is not passable to Tete from Mutarara so we must take this much longer route via Beira to get to Harare, Zimbabwe, our next destination.

The road from Caia to Beira is indescribable! All 300 kilometers of it is the worst I have seen it. There are huge holes, too many to count! We have a flat on the right front tire. I stop before it gets ruined. There is a roadside tire mender at a market and he repairs it. He has no fancy electric tools, only the basic ones. I discover that I forgot my tire wrench with the man who checked the bearing at Mutarara. The Lord has been helping us and the bearing has not given out. In fact, it even has cooled down! Thank you, Lord! It's a miracle that we have come this far.

It takes a while before we are back on the road. We finally reach the tarmac road at dark. When we reach Beira, we stop in at Baltazar's place. He is not at home but his son assists us to find a lodging place in town. Chitui, Chomanika, Don and I are finally safe and sound in our rooms. We thank the Lord for bringing us here safely! We could still be stranded in the middle of the Mozambican forest. We eat our evening meal and turn in.

It was nice to have slept in a clean bed and in a clean room. But this is not the day to sleep in. After a great breakfast, I take the vehicle to the garage. It takes hours before it is ready for me to drive. The bearing was not replaced. They said it is still good. It is a miracle how God took care of it! It is 4 P.M. before we are able to leave Beira behind us. Along the tarmac to Chimoio we come across many potholes due to the heavy rains. Water is standing everywhere because of the floods. Our churches in this area will need more assistance.

It is dark when we arrive and we book in at Moinho Motel for the night. They have made some improvements in it. A Portuguese couple is in charge now. After supper I finish my business with Chitui and with Chomanika. They are going on to Tete in the morning while Don Riley and I travel on to Harare, Zimbabwe.

*　　*　　*

Our missionary daughter Colleen is accompanying me on my next trip to Mozambique. It will be a treat to have her along—like old times when she traveled with us in Tanzania. Reinhard Berle and his nephew Thomas, plus Mario Hort with his son Isai, are coming along as well. Reinhard is the head of the Kinderhilfswerk work in Germany and has been a great help to us in Zambia and in Uganda. Mario is the pastor of a radio program in Brazil and speaks Portuguese fluently. At 6:30 A.M. we say goodbye to Marion and leave Lusaka for Mozambique. She will be preaching in the morning service here at Avondale.

We make proper time and before we reach Katete, we stop for our picnic lunch under a shady tree. After fuelling up at Katete, we turn south for Mozambique. We reach the border and find the Zambian officials out for lunch. It is half an hour before they make an appearance. On the Mozambican side, Mario and Isai begin using their Portuguese. Colleen takes over and drives the Nissan until we reach the bridge at Matundo. We find Chitui and his son Salvador sitting in front of their house. He informs us that he has booked us in at Tete Motel. We eat our supper on the patio overlooking the Zambezi River. A nice relaxing time after a long drive. Finally, it is time to turn in for the night.

Chitui shows up after breakfast and we all go to town. After purchasing a few things and filling up with fuel, we leave for Mutarara. Once we get onto the dirt road, we stop for a service at a place called Kambulatsitsi. The people have gathered in a large empty building. It is packed out and the children are all excited about meeting so many white people at one time. They sing heartily and after all the introductions and speeches, Mario shares the Word of God. Afterwards we leave. It is already very hot. To cool off, Thomas and Isai ride on top of the roof carrier. They enjoy all the attention given them from those we pass on the road.

Further down the road, we stop near Doa for another service. It is at Jeke Village. Here there is a time of singing and introductions as well. Colleen shares of her work in Uganda, and then Mario delivers the message. Before we can reach Mutarara, Chitui has another church for us to visit. This one is at Salima Village. The brick building is now completed. Again we sing and the one who has an instrument made from bicycle parts plays for us. It is one of a kind. After the introductions where we all share a few words, Mario preaches. By the time we leave it is four o'clock.

We drive like mad to get to Mutarara before dark but we fail. Chitui wants us to stop at another church but I refuse because of the lateness of the hour. It was to have been only one, but it has already turned out to be three! It is 6 P.M. when at long last we reach town. We run around in the dark hunting for a place that will house all of us. Finally, we settle for the old bat-infested hotel. It is not as smelly as before, but I do see one of them. Their water problem is still the same. We drive over to Piscina Restaurant for our supper. The woman is not around but her teenage children are. It takes them three hours to prepare the chicken, fish, rice, and potatoes! When we arrive back at the hotel, we have trouble finding any water for bathing. Quite a day we have had!

At 4:30 A.M. there is already a lot of activity outside our hotel: barking dogs, bleating goats, screaming babies, and rattling bicycles. I wait another hour before getting up. Someone brings us water from the river in a jerry can, so we are able to take a splash bath. With the river so near, they still have no water system installed that works in this hotel. Imagine! The flooded areas have mostly dried up and the tents are nearly all gone. We drive to Piscina Restaurant for our breakfast. The mother is present this morning but it still takes two and a half hours for her to prepare eggs, bread, and tea for us!

Our service today is at the grass-roofed church in Mutarara built right in the midst of large boulders. We must walk to it, as it is impossible to drive up to it with the Nissan. Many have gathered and the building is packed with many more standing outside. They sing for us and one even reads a prepared speech. After our greetings, Mario again preaches another fine message. He has been enjoying himself thus far, to be able to communicate with them in Portuguese. Of course, someone still has to translate it into Sena, the local language resembling Nyanja. Chomanika, who arrived yesterday evening from Malawi, translates for Reinhard, Colleen, and me when we share. Colleen is doing very well as she can to understand some of the Portuguese since she took Spanish in college. They are quite similar in many ways.

After the service, we try to find a new place to spend the night and find one right near the bridge with a nice view of the river. If I had known it yesterday that there was this place, I would have come here. The rooms are bare except for the bed. But they are much cleaner than what I have seen thus far in Mutarara. We immediately move over from the other hotel to this one. There are enough rooms here to go around for all. There is a slight problem with Colleen's room and mine. The locks on the doors do not work and I have to use the screwdriver to open them. Again, it takes a couple of hours to prepare a meal! Apparently this is how they do it here in Mozambique. It has been another hot day.

During the night, I hear one mosquito but it does not bother me. The group all have a good night of rest. We do not wait for breakfast, as we want an early start. Mario and Colleen buy biscuits, juice, and bottled water to eat along the way. It is a little after six when we start out for Tete. Chitui is traveling with us but Chomanika is returning to Nsanje, Malawi. When we reach Doa, we turn off the road and take a smaller one leading west towards the Zambezi River. It runs through a lot of heavy bush with only a few villages along the way. The road turns to the north when it nears the river. It is quite picturesque in some areas where we pass under the canopy of tall trees! Magnificent!

After driving 33 kilometers, we arrive at a remote village in a large clearing called Chague. It is my first time to be here. The people are friendly and happy to see us. We all gather inside the church they have built. It is packed full with many left standing outside. The front is crowded with children sitting on the dirt floor. Many of them are wearing charms around their necks. I do not dare move around too much or else I am liable to step on someone's fingers. There is a lot of singing before the introductions are made. All of us take our turns again. Mario once more is the preacher and he does an excellent job. As always we pray for those who come forward for salvation and healing.

There is no food for us before our departure. At all five churches where we have held services on this trip, we have not been served anything to eat or drink! Chitui has certainly not been teaching them about hospitality. On our return drive, before we get to Doa, we almost run over a man lying in the middle of the road. We discover he is dead drunk. There are several passersby who drag him off the road and we continue on our way. We arrive at the tarmac road without a further incident. The rest of the way to Tete is easy compared to where we just came from. We thank the Lord for His care and protection that He has given us on this trip thus far. It has been another hot day.

We check in at Tete Hotel, and they have rooms for all of us. Chitui returns to his home across the river. Colleen and I drive into town for a bit of shopping and to fill up with fuel. While sitting on the patio at the hotel sipping a cold soft drink, Isai comes dashing out of his room with the news that two jumbo jets have hit the Twin Towers of the World Trade Center in New York City, and as a result thousands have died! He had been watching the news on TV in Portuguese and this is what they are showing. We rush into his room and watch the unimaginable happening. It is mind-boggling! How can someone carry out this hideous act on innocent people? It is hard to believe that there can be hate of such magnitude!

The news is that another hijacked jumbo jet ploughed into the Pentagon at Washington, DC. A number of people are killed there as well. A fourth one crashes in Pennsylvania when some daring passengers over-power the hijackers. It was on its way to strike the White House. All this took place yesterday, September 11th, 2001. We are a day late in hearing this horrific news! While we were busily spreading the good news, there were acts of violence taking place on the other side of the world from us.

We are still in shock this morning over what has taken place in the States. Osama bin Laden has acknowledged that he is the one who masterminded this gruesome act that took place. President Bush has already declared war on him and his group called Al Qaeda. We take breakfast before leaving for Lusaka. Colleen does most of the driving. The Nissan has been overheating quite a bit the last two days so we do not speed. We reach the city at 6 P.M. Marion is waiting for us at Avondale.

Tomorrow, September 14, 2001, Colleen is leaving for Uganda. It has been a treat to have her with me for the past week in Mozambique. I started my ministry in Tanganyika (Tanzania) back in 1959 with her as a child at my side. Then in 1985, she joined me in Uganda, and now I am ending it with her at my side here in Southern Africa. Thank you, Lord, for this memorable time together! I could not have asked for a better ending to our walk together on the mission field in Africa.

Malawi

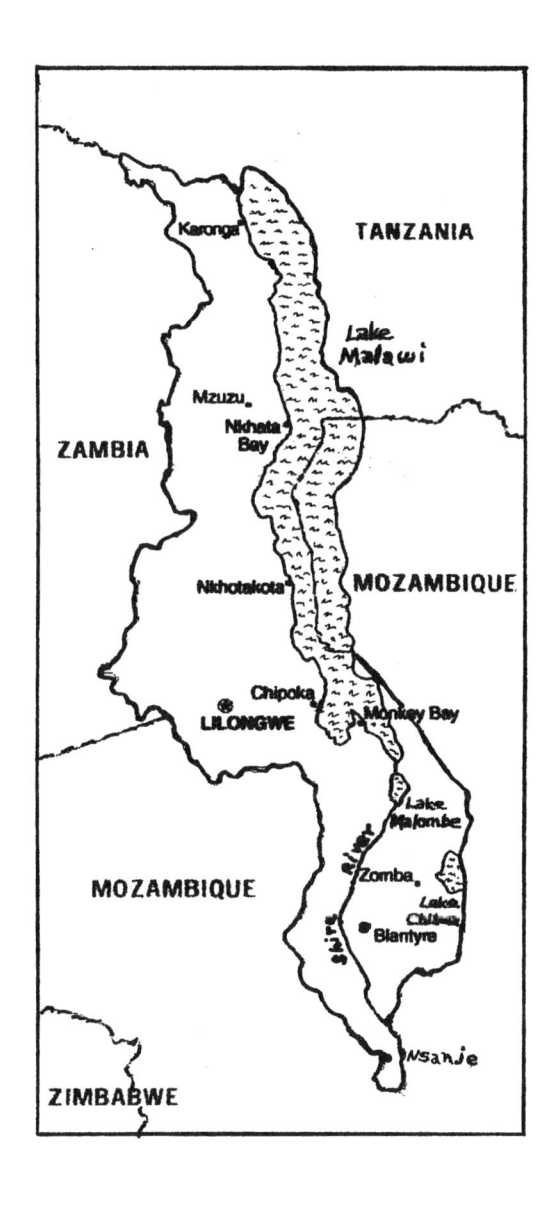

Ten
Planting Churches in Malawi

There is an earthquake at 4:40 A.M. January 20, 1995. This is the first one that we have experienced since coming to Zambia. It is a big one and lasts about 10 seconds. We are awakened by a rumbling sound that is immediately followed by a tremendous movement that rocks our bed. It reminds me of the ones we had at Kaiti Mission in Tanzania. Two days ago there was a big one in Japan and already 4,500 people are known to have died. It centered at Kobe, where Cheryl Johnson Barton and her husband Bernie are working as missionaries. I wonder how they fared through all this? Marion and I pack our clothes and leave at 6 A.M. for Malawi. We have prayer with the workers before we leave.

There had been an attempt made to establish the Church of God in Malawi several years earlier. But when we moved to Zambia and I tried to assist the work, we found there was no registration done with the Registrar of Society. In June 1994, Marion and I took Robert Edwards, the director for Africa, with us to check further into the condition of the work concerned. It was concluded that a new start would have to be made. And, so it is, that Marion and I are on a mission today to plant the church in Malawi. This means, first of all, finding someone in this country that will serve as our contact person until proper leaders can be trained.

Before we reach Katete we stop for tea and sandwiches that Marion brought along, as we did not have anything for breakfast. Lungu is traveling with us and will be going on ahead to Blantyre to alert a friend of his, whom he met on a previous trip, of our coming. Meanwhile, Marion and I drive on to Lake Malawi and book in at Livingstonia Beach Hotel. Tonight we talk about future plans of our life in Africa. Marion is resigning herself to retirement in Africa, even more than me it appears!

I have started going through my diaries looking for material to put into my next book. We have had a lot of experiences that we would forget, if I had not written them down. They bring back many fond memories. We had wonderful times with the kids. I will be writing again as soon as there is a lull in the work. Marion is reading a lot, mostly in the Bible. We also spend time talking about our future plans after retirement. Are we dreaming, or will it all come to pass?

A beautiful morning as the sun rises over the lake! It would be wonderful if we could stay on but duty calls us elsewhere. We leave at 8:30 A.M. and arrive in Blantyre at 3 P.M. The Presbyterian Church has a Conference Center with accommodations, and we book in at the Grace Bandawe guesthouse. Lungu and Joash, his Malawian acquaintance, show up in the evening and eat supper with us. A meeting is planned for the next day. It rains heavily after dark, so we turn in early.

The call for prayer by the Muslim cleric comes at 4 A.M.! We also hear howling dogs that join in, trying to copy him. Lungu and Joash eat breakfast with us. Afterwards, we meet those that have come for the conference. The teachings and discussions go well and most of them are interested in assisting us in establishing the church here. The paperwork begins and before the day is done, we take the *Constitution and Bylaws* over to the Registrar General. We are told that the final stage in registering the church will be done in Lilongwe, where the capital is situated. It has been a full day to say the least. There was plenty of rain again.

At nine this morning, I speak at a gathering here in Blantyre. I share on our doctrinal beliefs. There is a question and answer time afterwards. The Lord assisted me throughout the meeting. Marion and I have a break this afternoon so we do a little shopping. There is quite a bit of shooting tonight. It reminds us of our days spent in Kampala. In spite of the mattresses being only two inches thick, we have a fairly good rest. We return to the same place where I spoke yesterday. The building is full, 103 people have come out to the service. We start at ten and end at one o'clock. I pray for quite a few, and so does Marion. We also pray for the leaders who were appointed to help establish the church in Malawi. If they will allow the Holy Spirit to use them, we will see growth.

There is no food after the service, so we eat at Mount Soche Hotel. It is a nice change from rice and beef that we have been served twice a day at Grace Bandawe. At six this evening, we meet with Lungu and Joash. It is our last discussion with Joash as we leave in the morning. He is our contact person in Malawi.

We do not eat breakfast this morning, as we are tired of eggs and bread with tea. This is all they serve in the mornings. Before we can leave Blantyre, I need to get more Malawi Kwacha from the bank. It takes me two hours to get cash on my credit card! Lungu is returning with us to Zambia. We stop for a bite to eat at Lilongwe and then it is on to the border. We reach Lusaka before dark.

*   *   *

Seven weeks later, I am on my way back to Malawi to see how far things have come with the church. Marion is not with me but Lungu is. He will help me in teaching the new leaders concerning the structure and administration of the church. I will again teach on doctrine and theology. When we reach Blantyre, we book in at Grace Bandawe Center.

The following morning we meet at Nkhwangwala. (It means raven in the Chewa language.) It is a suburb of the city and hard to get to without a four-wheel drive. Over fifty have come to hear our teachings. It all goes well. The women do not serve food until evening. I close with an altar call and most of them come forward for prayer. It is already dark when I return to the center. I turn in without eating again. Tomorrow I carry on to Mozambique.

Marion comes with me on my next trip to Malawi. When we arrive in Lilongwe, I call Kirk's house to let them know of our arrival. Karen and the children come and direct us to their home. We are spending the night with them. It is September 14th, 1995, and Ashling's eighth birthday. There is a celebration tonight. Kirk is with UNICEF here in Malawi and stationed in Lilongwe. He was moved here from Uganda earlier this year.

Kirk is off to work right after breakfast so it is Karen who takes us shopping around town. As well, she takes me to check for TEE books in Nyanja at the Baptist Publishing House. We also visit Kirk at his office in the UN building. He has a nice view from his window. After lunching together, Marion and I leave for Blantyre. About 100 kilometers down the road the Nissan develops fuel problems. It sputters and loses power going up the hills.

121

It even stops altogether once. It must be the diesel I bought at Lilongwe. Should we return to Kirk's? We pray and ask the Lord to help us. And He does! We carry on and the vehicle acts up only once, just as we are entering the outskirts of the city.

We book in at Grace Bandawe Center. Among those who are waiting for us is Paffett Chomanika. I have not seen him for several years. It was back in 1989 when we met in Lusaka and discussed the prospects of working together in Malawi some day. Is this the day? Yes, he wishes to join us with his eight independent churches. He and Joash stay and eat supper with us while the rest go to their homes. I talk to them for a while before retiring for the night. It's been a full day again.

Chomanika and Joash show up for breakfast. We hunt for a place to clean the carburetor, and I am informed that it's not dirty! The fuel pump appears to be okay as well. So what is the problem? We return to the Grace Bandawe Center and hold a meeting with those who have come. I discuss the work with them and share on church administration. After a meal, we load our luggage into the vehicle and leave for Thyolo. But before we get there, we stop and hold a service on the outskirts of Limbe. Marion shares before I preach and then we pray for those who come up for help.

After booking in at the cheap motel in Thyolo, we travel a few more miles to start off the weekend seminar in an outdoor shelter. Marion again shares before my message. It is a good service with many accepting Christ. They feed us rice and chicken before we go back to the motel. It is after 7 P.M. and pitch dark. There are a lot of mosquitoes here tonight. This place is a hangout for noisy characters that love loud music and women. Not really a motel for missionaries to lodge in for the night.

We are both up until midnight killing mosquitoes, but still many more remain to annoy us. The wall is peppered with blood and dead ones! Finally, we give up and try to get some sleep. But we continue waking up a lot. We leave the only light in the room switched on, so as to keep them at bay. We get up at six o'clock. There is hot water for us in a small tub, so we take a wash of sorts. Marion and I have bread and tea for breakfast while the others add an egg each. The vehicle fared well during the night. We leave at 7:30 P.M. for the seminar. *A. M. ?*

I have a class for church leaders. Then, there is a service and it takes quite a long time before I get a chance to preach. Malawians love to sing, especially the women. Two headmen from nearby villages are present. Many come forward for prayer after the message. It is a good meeting! After a meal of rice and chicken again, Marion has a class with the women. I give out New Testaments before we head back to Blantyre. Marion and I have only tea for supper, while Chomanika and Joash have their rice and beef here at the Center.

I drop Chomanika off at the bus station. He is returning to Nsanje where he makes his home. Joash and I check at the registrar's office about the church registration. It is still in the processing stage. In Zambia it did not take this long to register the church. I return to the center for Marion and the luggage. Then we are off to Mozambique where we will spend some time with the work before returning to Zambia.

*   *   *

It is four months before I again return to Malawi. I am flying into Lilongwe on January 10, 1996, from Lusaka, and Kirk is there to pick me up at the airport. At his house I find Marion coming down with malaria, so I start her off on the curative Halfan. She has been staying with Kirk and his three girls for a month now filling in the gap that Karen has left with her untimely death. It is nearly two months now since our beloved Karen lost her life as a result of a road accident. I have shared this tragic event in my previous book *Long Shadows,* chapter nineteen; therefore, I will not go into it again.

I do want to add this, that I met Karen for the last time, a month before her accident, on the Great East Road as I was returning home from a seminar in Eastern Province. Kirk and his family had just spent a few days with Marion and were returning to Malawi when we met on the road and stopped to visit for a while. None of us knew at that time what would take place just thirty-one days later and would so jolt our family!

Marion is still in much pain from the accident that she, herself, was in ten days ago. The therapist says that she has a cracked breastbone as well from hitting the steering wheel, besides the sore neck and bruised arm. We were returning from Lake Malawi, where we all had gone for a vacation, when she lost control of Kirk's vehicle that she was driving and drove off the road. The car went down a steep grade, across a furrow in the field, and over a termite mound before stopping in front of a hut. It is a miracle that no one inside the vehicle was severely hurt! Natasha, Shaina, Mikaela, and Emma the babysitter were with Marion in the car.

Mikaela is still not walking by herself even though her cast was removed a week ago. A therapist comes daily to work on her leg. Since my arrival, she likes to be with her Opa, which is grandpa in German. Shaina is faring well while Ashling has started school and is gone all afternoon. Marion has chills and does a lot of sweating during the night. In the morning she feels somewhat better. But then by afternoon she has chills again, and in the evening she is unable to keep down her supper. She has really been having it rough! Besides looking after three children while in pain from the accident, she now has to contend with malaria. "Lord, continue to grant her strength and restore her to full health. Amen."

Marion has another restless night. She sweats a lot and has chills on and off. I must travel to Blantyre and check on the progress of work. At nine, I am ready to leave. It rains some along the way. When I arrive, I find Grace Bandawe Center full so I have to find another lodging place. I discover the Baptist Guesthouse is empty, so I book a room for three nights. Three of the leaders show up and we talk about the work until late. The following two days I meet with all the leaders at a church that we rent for this occasion and I share more of the Word of God with them. In closing, we hold a meeting to discuss the future of the work in Malawi.

It takes a while before I find a place that will repair my flat tire. As soon as it is done, Joash and I start on our journey to Nsanje. It takes some time to descend the Thyolo escarpment as it has many hairpin curves and switchbacks. The view of the Shire Valley below us is beautiful! This year the Shire River has flooded its banks in several places. The final 50 kilometers of our journey has dips in the road with swift running water passing over most of them. If the water had been any deeper, I would not have chanced going through them. When we arrive at Nsanje, we find that it had rained here heavily. There is water still standing everywhere.

People show up after dark and I share the Word of God. It is after 8 P.M. when we end the service. I am sleeping in Chomanika's house tonight. The bed I am given has weak springs and makes a noise each time I move. There are so many mosquitoes about that Chomanika gives me a lighted coil to burn in my room. The coil gives off an odor that is supposed to keep the mosquitoes at bay. But it does not seem to help. I wake up a lot throughout the night and I am forced to use my insect spray. But more just keep coming!

In the morning I have a nice wash in a cement enclosure. It is strange that Africans expect me to squeeze into their narrow latrines, but they themselves use the outdoor showers that are much easier to enter! The result is that all their showers smell of urine. There is bread and tea for breakfast. Then I teach for two hours on the Church. After this I preach and many seek the Lord in prayer. In closing, I pass out Bibles to the church leaders. It is very hot inside the building and I am all wet by the time we are through.

Paffett's wife feeds us before we start on our journey to another newly planted church. The dips on the road that were running with water yesterday are now dry. We turn off the road before we reach Chikwawa and drive west to the village of Mtuwa. The trail gets worse and worse before we finally arrive at the village surrounded by hills. Let us hope that it will not rain tonight or we may not get back to the main road!

We go into the service right away. After my message, only old people come forward for healing. That's different! We eat afterwards. There are lots of flies around because of the livestock. I have a teaching session yet tonight under the trees. The choirs sing for us and are still singing when I turn in for the night. I am again given a bed with springs. It was hot and humid all day. No mosquitoes tonight, so I am keeping the windows open on my room. I have to tell the church leader here to shut down the choirs, as they are still singing at 11:30 P.M.!

I have a wash this morning as it is much needed for I did a lot of sweating during the night. Breakfast consists of rice and tea. The service commences just as dark clouds start to roll in. For musical instruments, the women are shaking cans that contain small pebbles. They make a loud rattling noise. (They had them at Nsanje as well.) There are two men who are beating drums. After my sermon, I take time to pray for those who come forward. When I am done, the rain starts to come down. We rush to the vehicle and take leave without the usual shaking of hands.

The trail is now slippery because of the rain. At one place I have to skirt around a large gap in the road that the running water was washing even wider. At another place a concrete crossing was breaking apart and I have only enough space for the wheels to cross it! The Lord sees us through safely back to the main road. Thank you, Lord! It rains all the way back to Blantyre. I unload Joash at his house and carry on to the Baptist Guesthouse. After a bath, I retire for the night. I think again of Karen's death. Why did it have to happen? "Why, Lord?"

In the morning I load the vehicle, eat my breakfast, and then leave for Lilongwe. Marion is happy to see me, and so are the three girls. I sit around chatting and playing with my granddaughters all afternoon. They act like they are our own kids! Marion has been their mother since Karen's death. Kirk makes an appearance at 6 P.M. I talk to him for some time after the children go off to bed. He still cries for Karen and misses her tremendously. We weep together. It is good for both of us, as he hasn't really opened up to me since her death. Marion joins us after she has tucked in the children and we talk until 10 P.M.

I spend four more days with Marion, Kirk, and his girls in Lilongwe before returning to Lusaka. During this time I check on the church registration. I am told that it should be out next week. I spend quality time with Shaina and Mikaela while Ashling is at school. Marion says that Ashling often cries herself to sleep because of missing her mom. She told her that it was hard for her at Christmas time. All her cousins could say, "Mommy, look what I got!" but she couldn't. UNICEF has agreed to move Kirk to Lusaka so that he and his girls can be near family. So there is a lot of packing to be done. I take a load of breakable items back with me in the Nissan. Marion will come later with the girls by plane.

Reinhard Berle and Tim Stevenson visit us in April and I am now taking them to Malawi where we want to check on the registration of Kinderhilfswerk, an organization from Germany that is helping us with the work in Zambia. It is Reinhard's wish that he can assist the church as well in Malawi with relief work, boreholes, and orphans. Along the way we stop at Katete for a service where they both share and orphans are given their quarterly allotment. There are quite a few here who are sponsored by those in Germany through Kinderhilfswerk.

After a night in a nearby motel we return to Songwe for a service and Tim delivers the message. There are over 500 people present. We pray for those who come forward, including a woman who is oppressed by demons. Afterwards, all three of us are showered with gifts of groundnuts, bananas, pumpkins, and a live chicken. They also feed us before we start off for Malawi. Before crossing the border, we turn off at Chipata and drive to the place where Karen had her accident. No trace of the fatal mishap remains. We finally reach Lilongwe and check in at the Golden Peacock. It is 10 P.M. before we retire to our rooms after having an excellent time of sharing stories.

We check on the registration of Kinderhilfswerk and learn that the certificate should be forthcoming in a couple of weeks. We also take a look at the vehicle that Karen was in when it was hit by the lorry. It is irreparable! It takes another day before we can start out for Lusaka. When we do, we also take back with us Kirk's car that had been left behind for repairs.

*   *   *

A month later, I enter southern Malawi from Mutarara, Mozambique. This time Moyo is with me. We reach Nsanje and find Chomanika waiting for us. We sit around and talk until dark before food is served. Afterwards there is a service where Moyo brings the message. I retire in the vehicle and sleep on the back seats. The others are sleeping in Chomanika's house along with the goats that are occupying one of the rooms! It is hot inside the Nissan with the windows closed, but there are mosquitoes out there so I do not dare open them.

I make out fairly well in spite of not having a mattress or sleeping bag. Toward morning when it gets cooler, I drape my jacket over me. It is early when the people start moving about the compound. Those that did not sleep inside the church, slept outside on the ground. We have tea and a *mandazi* (fritter) before the service at 8:30 A.M. While waiting for people to come forward after my message, there are two who show signs of demon possession. I walk over to the one who is shaking and when I place my hand on her shoulder, the demons manifest themselves. It takes only a few minutes to cast them out of her. While I am dealing with her, a second person starts acting up. I go to her, after I am done with the first person, and it does not take long to drive these out as well.

There are twenty-six children who need to be dedicated. This I do after we observe the Lord's Supper. Give out Bibles, TEE books, and religious material before it is time to eat. We had 221 villagers attend this weekend seminar. Now it is off to Ngombe Village in Chikwawa District where 164 have gathered for the service. After my sermon I pray for those who come forward, plus for the twenty-three children who are being dedicated to the Lord. I also give out Bibles, TEE books, and literature here as well. When finished, we return to Blantyre and check in at Grace Bandawe. Chomanika and Moyo are also staying here.

I sleep well. For breakfast I take tea and bread but refuse the eggs, as I'm not in the mood for any more of them. It takes an hour and a half to get money at the bank with my credit card! There is a meeting with the leaders at the center that lasts most of the day. Some write their TEE tests afterwards. I pass out songbooks, and two bicycles to the district leaders of Nsanje and Chikwawa.

On my way back to Lilongwe, I am asked to hold a service at Nkaya Village in Machinga District. We turn off the tarmac road and drive east into bush country. After driving 25 kilometers on a dirt road that keeps deteriorating the further we travel, I reach a furrow that cuts across it. There is not enough time to scout for a way around it, as I need to get to Lilongwe to shop for TEE books before closing time. I turn the Nissan around and make my way back to the tarmac road, leaving one of the leaders behind to look after the service.

Along the way a helicopter shows up and flies by me overhead. It turns around and swoops alongside me low enough for me to see the pilot. I am sure he reads the name of our church on the side of the Nissan. He is probably wondering who is driving out here in the bush with a Zambian registered vehicle? And a white man at that! The helicopter churns up dust all around me as it hovers just above the ground. Will he stop me for questioning? I keep driving slowly. Finally, it gains altitude and flies off. That was scary!

Before we reach Lilongwe, we come across several Nyao dancers on their way to a traditional ceremony. They smear white paint on their faces and bodies. One looks like an animal. They generate a fearsome sight! We check in at the Golden Peacock where Reinhard, Tim, and I stayed a month ago. This place is one of those guest-houses where you can hear everything all the way down the hall. What someone says, when someone coughs, or whatever! The bathroom is very unclean and smelly.

After breakfast, Moyo and I check at the Ministry of Justice for the church's registration and I am informed that it is done. It has been sent to our church's address in Blantyre. I learn that Kinderhilfswerk's registration will take another week. Our work done, we leave for Zambia. The border crossing takes no time at all. At Katete, I drop off Moyo and carry on to Lusaka. Marion has a nice supper waiting for me. We talk until 11 P.M.

I travel to Malawi two different times after this in order to hold meetings with the leaders. All goes well and I restock their supply of Bibles and songbooks. Several write their TEE tests. Paffett Chomanika is the now the

National Church Representative. I assist the flood-stricken area in the lower Shire Valley where the river swept away houses and crops. There were several villagers who lost their lives. They are receiving bags of maize from our relief fund. After two years of hard work and a passion for souls, there are now eighty-two churches with 6,896 members in Malawi.

Who will be the first to give way?

Carrying their produce to market

When bikes are too small, there is the ox-cart.

Selling roasted field mice alongside the road

Don Riley, Chomanika, and another flat tire

Many possessions were lost during the floods.

Not one, but two flats are repaired!

Homes destroyed by floodwaters

Baby with mother bringing
home firewood

"A good catch of field
mice, boys!"

Soon to join big sister in
worshipping God

A leper who has already
lost fingers and toes

One of many churches in Malawi

Worshipping the Lord

Bean-filled cans serve as musical instruments.

Paffett Chomanika receives his ordination.

Angolan worshippers include the border officials.

Border officials at Angolan border crossing

Jim and Dulci Doty are my contacts in Luanda.

My only way to get to Luanda is by air.

This large fort in Luanda overlooks the Atlantic Ocean.

Cannons lie silent today on top of the old fort.

A worship service is held next to a building at Viana.

Joao Antonio translates for me.

Dulci Doty plays with the youth group at Viana.

Another congregation near Viana

Here we are sharing the Word of God in a service.

Jose Barros receives his Certificate of Ordination.

The entrance to Moffat Mission near Kuruman

Tim and Chief Mukuni stand with me where Livingstone once stood.

The garden where Livingstone courted Mary

Inside the palace of Chief Mukuni

I stand perched at the rim of Victoria Falls on Livingstone Island.

Grave of Mary Livingstone at Shupanga Mission

A statue of Livingstone overlooks Victoria Falls.

This is the old fort at Tete, where Livingstone often stopped.

The house where Livingstone stayed in Zanzibar

The place where Stanley found Livingstone in Ujiji

The site where Livingstone died at Chitambo Village

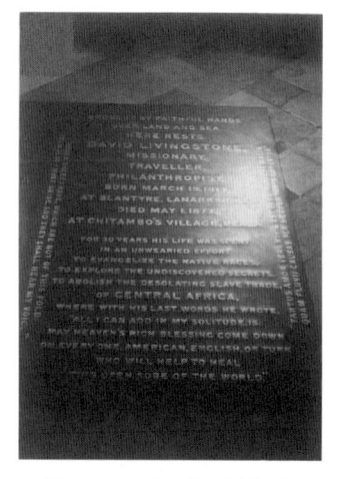

Plaque on tomb at West-minster Abbey, London

I pose with Norman Carr at his camp near the Luangwa River.

Where did Tiffany inherit those writing skills?

Jane Goodall appears at a function in Lusaka.

I finally meet Fred Holland, the founder of TEE.

Jakobsh, Roesler, and Sommert visit us as well.

Helga Stalts and Oscar Ndao treat patients.

Doug and Frieda Karau travel with us in Zambia.

Warren Senft assists us in district seminars.

Eleven
The Shire River Floods

When I reach Blantyre, I head for the bank to purchase some Malawi Kwacha with my credit card. As usual I am told to check back in two hours, as that is how long it will take to process the transaction. I have enough local cash with me for a meal, so I drop in at the nearby hotel. When I return for my money, the teller informs me that my credit card has been declined. So I hand him another one. I am told to return tomorrow, as he will not know the answer in time before closing hours. I leave and check in at the Baptist Guesthouse. Take a hot bath and turn in for the night.

After breakfast at the hotel, I walk over to the bank and discover my second request for money has been accepted. I then drive over to Grace Bandawe and find Chomanika waiting for me. We talk about the work and its needs. I purchase two bikes for the district leaders at Milange and Phalombe. Songbooks are needed but the bookshop is out of them. I call Marion at Livingstone and talk to her for a while. I inform her of my fall from the vehicle in Mozambique. She herself is okay. Colleen e-mailed her that they had a severe thunderstorm at Kampala that wiped out a lot of their electrical equipment.

I do not sleep too well. There are too many thoughts

running through my head. Today, I meet with the Executive Committee. Joash is not present, as he has left the church. It is 9:30 P.M. before we quit for the night. The following morning, we carry on with our meeting. The work needs reviving, so I share for some time before we conclude at noon. Hand out TEE books, Bibles, and tracts to the leaders after our meal at Grace Bandawe. We then go looking for a plot where the central church will one day be built but do not find a suitable site. The Executive Committee is to keep searching further.

This evening I am able to raise my head while lying on my back for the first time since my fall. I am still sore in my lower back and stiff in my neck but am improving gradually. It is a miracle that I am not in any worse shape! I could have broken some bones or suffered internal injuries. I think of Marion tonight. I miss her and long for her. We have not been together much lately. It's been eleven days since I left home on this trip, and it will be another eleven days before I see her again! This journey has taken me to Mozambique and Malawi, with Zimbabwe still to be done.

I leave Blantyre after breakfast and head north for Lilongwe. When I arrive, I stop and visit Tim's parents Gerald and Ellen Stevenson, missionaries for the PAOC (Pentecostal Assemblies of Canada) here in Malawi. It is nice to see them again and I end up spending the night with them. In the morning I am given breakfast before I start out for Zambia. After crossing the border, I stop at the police station in Chipata to find out what happened to the truck driver that had hit Karen's vehicle and brought about her death. I am told that he was released after paying a fine.

The road between Katete and Petauke is full of potholes and craters that slow me down to a crawl. I hit one of them after I cross the Luangwa River and the back tire goes flat. Replace it with the spare and carry on to Lusaka without a further mishap. Then, it is on to Zimbabwe.

*   *   *

On my following trip to Malawi, I am taking Oscar Ndao along to assist me. When we reach Lilongwe, we book in at a Korean guesthouse. After eating at their restaurant, we turn in for the night. In the morning, Oscar and I leave for Blantyre and arrive at noon. Today it takes me three and a half hours at the bank to get some money with my credit card. The longest ever! We travel to Ngabu, where Chomanika teaches in a nearby school. I catch up on the progress of the work. We chat till dark. The electricity goes on and off until we retire at 8:30 P.M. Mosquitoes are around, so I hang the net over the bed I am sleeping in. Oscar does the same with his bed. Several fleas have already bitten me from sitting on the stuffed chairs.

Someone died nearby so there is singing all night beside the dead man's hut. They are Christian songs. As soon as the wailing starts, the singers interrupt them with their songs. This carries on until mid afternoon when finally they bury the young man who died of AIDS. Today we are checking various sites where Kinderhilfswerk can assist the villagers with boreholes but find they already have one or two of them at each village we travel to.

In the evening, we end up at Nsanje for a service but the people first show up at 9:30 P.M., when Oscar and I have turned into our tents for the night. This does not stop them from singing and they carry on until past midnight. I finally send Chomanika to quiet them down. It is just too loud! Because of the singing, I sleep only four hours. I finally get up at 4:30 A.M. and take a shower. There is a breakfast of rice again before the service at 6:30. We pray for those who come forward, and then make our way back to Blantyre.

We have a good night at Grace Bandawe with no mosquitoes. After breakfast we hold the Executive Committee meeting. We discuss numerous issues. Oscar contributes a lot. At one o'clock, the meeting closes and we leave for Lilongwe without eating. Drop Oscar off at the Korean guesthouse and I go on to Mark's place where I visit and spend the night with them. The following day, Mark accompanies Oscar and me to Lusaka.

I fly into Blantyre from Harare for my next visit. Chomanika is there to pick me up with a taxi. We drive into town and book in at Grace Bandawe. Most of the other Executive Committee members are present and we discuss the work until 8:30 P.M. with a break for supper. We do not finish our business so we meet again in the morning after breakfast consisting of eggs and bread. It is late in the evening before we can conclude our discussions. There was a break at noon for lunch. Each meal I have eaten chicken and rice. Some of the others order beef and *nsima*. I forgot to bring along a towel so I end up drying my face with my red bandana. The towel they have given me here is quite smelly and frayed. Imagine, a worn out towel for their guests!

I pick up a few fleabites during the night. Today we drive out in a taxi to inspect a piece of property, but again it is not a suitable site for a central church in Blantyre. I wait two hours for money at the bank. So what's new? The exchange rate presently is 40 Malawi Kwacha to a U.S. dollar. I buy a towel, insect spray, and bottled drinking water. I have been moving around on foot, even walking to town from the center. I need the exercise. This evening I continue to jot down notes for my next book. I would like to really get going on it. It is long overdue. But the pressure of the work does not leave me much free time.

After my breakfast here at the center, a taxi takes me to the airport where I board my flight back to Harare. The plane inside is in need of some maintenance. The toilet door hangs on just one hinge and cannot be closed properly. I have to hang onto the handle while inside! I discover two dead cockroaches that got trapped inside the two windowpanes beside my seat. How did they get in there? A taxi drives me to my hotel when I reach Harare.

*   *   *

Three months later, I am returning to Malawi where there has been rioting at Blantyre since the election a week ago. Ten mosques have been burned to the ground, plus a shop, and a home. Windscreens on government vehicles were also smashed. I am trusting that it will be peaceful when I get there. Afunika Tembo and Mailes Ndao are catching a ride to Eastern Province and drop off along the way. I drive nonstop and reach Blantyre after dark. It takes me twelve hours to clock 1,010 kilometers. I find Chomanika waiting for me at Grace Bandawe Center and we check in. It has been a long day behind the wheel, and yet I do not feel too bad. Thank you, Lord, for a safe trip!

This morning I have a rude awakening when I almost brush my teeth with shaving cream instead of toothpaste! I discover a flat on the Nissan when I get ready to drive to town. Replace it with the spare and then get the tire repaired. Buy a box of Chewa Bibles and 100 songbooks for the work. Call Marion and talk to her for a few minutes.

Send a postcard off to Tiffany. It is her thirteenth birthday today, June 25, 1999. In the afternoon, I get together with the leaders that have already arrived for the Executive Committee meeting.

We meet again the following day. It finally ends in the evening. It has been decided that Paffett Chomanika will represent Malawi at the World Conference next month in Great Britain. There are now 110 churches with 15,411 members. We are now in all three Regions: Southern, Central, and Northern. In the morning I leave for Tete, Mozambique, taking Chomanika along to translate for me.

My next trip to Malawi takes longer than usual because of the roads. There are potholes galore! They are very hard on the vehicle. I reach Lilongwe after dark and drop in at Gerald and Ellen Stevenson's for the night. We visit until late. I leave in the morning for Blantyre. Along the way I come across young men selling field mice that have been roasted. They have them stuck onto the ends of sticks, much like a wiener. I ask him to sample one for me and he does. Zambians love them as well. What about me? Nope! I do not buy any of them.

I want to check into the Baptist Guesthouse this trip but they are full. So I end up again at Grace Bandawe Center. I wanted a change as I got bitten up too much by fleas last time. Will I escape them this time? Chomanika shows up and we discuss the work. We plan to travel to Mozambique tomorrow just as soon as Chitui shows up.

We leave for Milange and when we reach the border, Chomanika discovers he did not bring along his passport. The officials will not permit him to cross into Mozambique without it. It is senseless to go on without him, as Chitui does not speak English. A real disappointment! Here I am traveling with two national leaders and yet I am unable to do what I had planned. It reminds me of the three stooges!

I decide to hold a service at one of the churches near the border in Malawi before turning back to Blantyre. The pastor is informed that we plan to be there in the morning. Meanwhile we are spending the night in a motel here at Mulanje. It is a cheapie with only one toilet and one sink in the whole place!

It is quite congested this morning and I do not get to shave because of the long line up at the washroom. I end up taking a wash at the tap outside. We have eggs for breakfast. What else is new! Our service is at Soza Village. There is no grass on the church roof, so it is very hot inside. The top of my head is getting enough sun today. At least 100 are present and after my message, many come forward for salvation and healing. The pastor's wife gives me two stocks of bananas before we leave. When we reach Blantyre, I finish my business with Chomanika and Chitui as I plan to start my journey back to Zambia tomorrow.

Leave early and on the way to Lilongwe, I come across more young fellows selling dried mice on spikes. I am spending the night with the Stevensons again. It is an enjoyable evening; we even talk to Colleen and Tim by phone. I leave for Lusaka in the morning and reach it by dark.

I return to Malawi three months later. The work is steadily growing and there are now 135 congregations. I spend three days here before moving on to Mozambique to fulfill what I had planned on my previous visit. After three days in that country, I return and spend three more days in Malawi. I call Marion from Blantyre and wish her a happy Valentine's Day, it being February 14, 2000. She is preparing a birthday party for Mark when I get back home in two days' time.

While traveling on to Lilongwe the front tire blows! I have no trouble keeping the Nissan on the road. Both the tire and tube are ruined. Some villagers assist me in removing the flat tire and putting on the spare. Twenty kilometers later I come across cattle that are wandering onto the road! The herder makes no attempt to stop them. I slam on the brakes but still smash into one of them. The bull bar in front of my Nissan protects the headlights from getting broken and the fender from getting bent. A miracle! The cow hobbles off the tarmac holding up one of its hind legs. I watch it for a while before carrying on to Lilongwe. It should be okay as none of the bystanders came charging up to my vehicle.

I buy a tire and tube and have them mounted before dropping in at the Stevensons for a visit and to spend the night with them again. I will be back in Lusaka tomorrow.

*   *   *

Three months later, I fly into Blantyre from Zimbabwe. Chomanika meets me at the airport with a rented car. We will be using it to get around on my trip this time. After cashing some money, we leave for his place at Ngabu in the Shire Valley where we hold a service yet just as it is getting dark. Over 100 are present. There is lots of singing again afterwards. I am staying in the same room I slept in before. Lots of mosquitoes around again, but I have brought along some spray to use on them. I am given a pillow but I do not use it.

Up at 6 A.M. and have a splash bath heated by Paffett's wife. Then it is eggs for breakfast with bread and tea. The service starts at eight o'clock with about 100 in attendance. Many respond after my message and come up for prayer. I assist several orphans and widows with maize, as they are some of the poorest of the poor in this area. On our way to Nsanje, we turn off the road and drive to a place near the Shire River where several homes and a church were destroyed by floodwaters. There are six churches in all that will need assistance to rebuild. I am leaving funds for this project with Chomanika and Thole, the District Chairman, to oversee the building of them.

Before we reach Nsanje, we stop at Chiromo and eat at a place called Half London. There was a restaurant in Kampala, Uganda, by that name as well, only fancier! We meet two lads carrying an armful of mice they had just caught with their father. Others are still digging alongside the road for them. At Nsanje, we hold a service with those who have been waiting for us since forenoon. About 100 are present to hear my sermon. Again many respond to the message. There are eight churches here that will need help to rebuild. I book in for the night at Discovery Motel near Nsanje.

I really got dirty yesterday as we drove with our windows open, due to no air conditioner in the rented vehicle. My shirt collar is filthy! I'm thankful for the warm water they bring me, as there is only cold water in the taps. I meet with the group at the church and we discuss the needs brought about by the Shire River overflowing its banks and flooding much of the area. There are orphans and widows here that I assist by taking them to the market place and purchasing clothing and maize for them. I also pay for the orphans' school fees. Three of the leaders receive bicycles.

When we reach Blantyre, Chomanika and I check in at the center. I remove the woollen blankets from my bed, as that is where the fleas love to congregate. After a shower to wash off the dust, I turn in. Tomorrow, I will catch my flight back to Harare. In the morning I wake up itchy from fleabites! I just cannot make a trip to Malawi or Mozambique without picking up their bites. It is because of sleeping in these cheap guesthouses in order to save funds for the work of God.

* * *

After making several more visits to Malawi to check on the work, Don Riley, the Regional Director for Africa, is traveling with me on this trip. In fact, we will be going not only to Malawi, but also to Mozambique and Zimbabwe as well to meet some of the leaders. We stop at Lilongwe for the night and then carry on to Blantyre in the morning. When we arrive, we check in at Grace Bandawe Center where our Executive Council will be meeting. After the noonday meal, the meeting starts. Reports are given and the amended *Constitution and By-laws* are passed. Don speaks to the group before we pray for the Executive Council members. I give out Bibles and tracts to them before we eat.

The following day, I purchase five bicycles for new District Overseers, plus tires and tubes for those that still have their bikes. I look up Fred Holland who is presently in Malawi. He is the editor of the Theological Education by Extension program. I have been using the TEE books extensively ever since 1984 when we started training pastors in Uganda. The program has helped us immensely to keep up with the rapid growth we are experiencing in all the countries we are presently working in. It is a privilege to finally meet him. He is presently teaching a course at the Evangelical Bible College in Blantyre.

In our service at Ngabu, Chomanika receives his First Course Certificate in TEE. He also is ordained before Don Riley brings the message. Many come forward praying for help from the Lord. Before we leave, I assist twelve churches with relief funds here in Chikwawa District. There is a scarcity of food because of floodwaters destroying their crops. The back tire on the Nissan is ruined on our way to Nsanje. When we get there, we find people already waiting for us. Don preaches again. Here in this district, I give out relief to seven churches.

We sleep at the Discovery Motel where I have stayed a few times before. In the morning I find someone who can change the tire that got wrecked yesterday with the extra tire and tube I brought along. It is a good thing I did! The road has really deteriorated because of the heavy rains and it takes us over an hour to reach the Mozambican border.

My last trip to Malawi is September 1, 2001. My flight from Harare arrives in Blantyre at 1:30 P.M. Chomanika is there with a taxi and we end up at Grace Bandawe where we check in for two nights. I wonder how many fleabites I will pick up this time? It will be their last chance to get at me since I will not be returning here again. A sobering thought—I shall not pass this way again!

We talk about the work until it is time to eat. Then after prayer, we retire to our rooms. Before crawling into bed, I remove the woollen blanket from beneath the sheet that they have the habit putting on top of the mattress. In fact, I end up making one bed out of the two. I use both mattresses, as one is so thin that I can feel the boards underneath it. The bottom sheets of both beds are dirty so I use the top ones. The pillowcases are also dirty, not washed since the last person slept on them! I turn one of them inside out and use it. To top it off, I hear rats running around in the attic! They are very noisy. This center has really gone down from what I remember it to be when first I started coming here.

For two days, Chomanika and I carry on discussing the work. It is growing satisfactorily. I trust it will continue to do so after I leave Africa. There are presently 169 churches with 28,248 members in Malawi. Will someone who follows me have the same passion for souls as I have had? My flight back to Harare goes as scheduled. Marion is waiting for me at the airport. We return to Livingstone the following day.

Angola

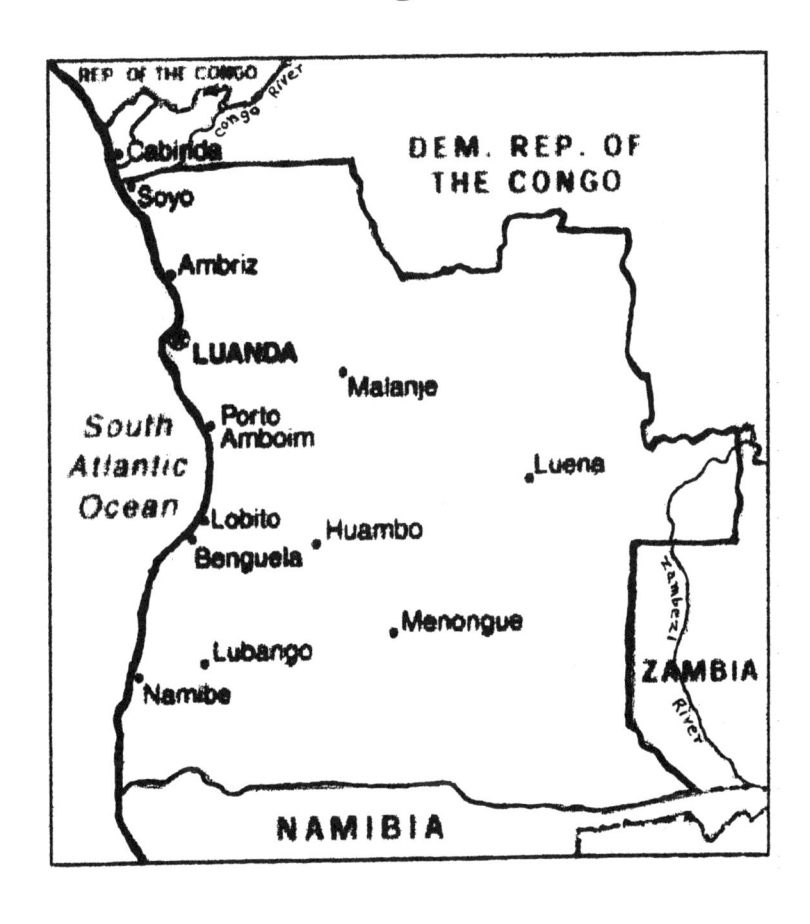

Twelve
Journeys to Angola

I am holding seminars in North-Western Province and, while at Kakhoma Village in Kavuma District, I drive over to Chingi on the Angolan border. It is April 10, 1995. Christians from the Zambian side of the border have started three congregations among their kin and I want to meet some of the believers. At the border post, the Zambian officials will not allow me to drive across the border with my vehicle. They inform me there are landmines that have been planted on the road we must use in order to reach Cazombo where the first church is located. So I park the Nissan Patrol and we commence our walk across the border. David Leyo, the regional leader for North-Western Province is with me.

A guide walks with us to meet the Angolan officials. He warns us to stay on the footpath and not step off it, as landmines are scattered around in the whole area. We follow him faithfully in single file. The officials we meet are with the rebel movement UNITA under Savimbi. Others appear from the nearby huts and join us. I share the Lord and pray with them. In the end, I give them Portuguese literature and a Bible. The Immigration officer is the pastor at this church! I visit with them for a while longer before returning to the Zambia side and my vehicle.

My desire is that soon I will be able to travel freely in

Angola and establish the church in that country. I am told that by August the government and UNITA will agree to disarm the soldiers and clear away the landmines. The men we have just met do not want war. But the war does not end. Peace treaty after peace treaty is signed and before the ink is dry they are broken!

We keep contact with the Angolan churches across the border, helping them with Bibles and literature. But it is almost four years before I learn of someone who will assist me to register the church in the capital city, Luanda. It takes me months to acquire a visa from the Angolan Embassy in Lusaka to enter their country.

January 8th 1999, I leave the Nissan at Kirk's place here in Lusaka and Mark drives me out to the airport. The Angolan Airliner TAAG is supposed to leave at 12:30 P.M. but it is late by an hour and a half. I am the only white person on this flight. This aircraft looks beautiful on the outside but the inside of it looks just the opposite! It is in need of a paint job and some repairs. The foam on the seats is worn thin and the backs of those that are empty flop forwards when we land at Harare an hour later. Several passengers disembark. When we are on our way again, a fly has joined us for this leg of the flight. The meal they serve us is tasty.

The plane lands at 6:30 P.M. their time, which is an hour behind ours in Zambia. In spite of arriving an hour and a half late, I find Jim Doty still waiting at the Luanda airport for me. He takes me to his house where I will be staying a week. I meet his wife Dulci who is Brazilian and speaks very little English. Jim is employed with the oil company Chevron and has been in correspondence with me concerning the registration of the church here in Angola. She serves us a big meal for supper. Before going to bed, I send Marion an e-mail to let her know of my safe arrival.

I spend the forenoon talking with Jim while his wife attends some meeting. She has helped to plant several churches for the group that she was affiliated with before marrying Jim. They met several years ago up in Cabinda where he had been stationed before coming down to Luanda. In the afternoon, they take me for a drive to see the city and the Atlantic Ocean. Oil rigs stand just off-shore in the harbor. There is a large fortress built by the Portuguese overlooking the ocean. Their large cannons lie silent today. I am also taken to see his office where he works with computers for Chevron.

Tonight Jim calls his father in Texas and I talk with him for a while. Marion met him when she went to speak at Gulf Coast Bible School in Houston, where he was the dean at that time. She had gone there during mission's emphasis week. This was during the years when I was the pastor at Carstairs, Alberta.

I go along with the Dotys to attend the service this Sunday morning at one of the evangelical churches here in Luanda. It is all in Portuguese except for some of the choir numbers that are in KiKongo, one of the tribal languages in upper Angola. I understand a lot of their words, as it is one of the many Bantu dialects found across Africa. I meet someone after the service that may be assisting our church here in Angola. His name is Romiro. There is someone else coming in from Cabinda who also is interested. His name is Jose Barros. Dulci knows both of them very well. This evening I talk with the Dotys about the registration of the church in Angola.

In the morning there is an e-mail from Marion and all is well back home. Jim has to be at his office, so I go to town with his driver who speaks English. I check on my return flight and discover that it is full on Friday! They have overbooked the flight. I am to check back on Wednesday. Hopefully, there will be a cancellation. So much for buying a return ticket! I cash some dollars into their local currency and I am shocked at the exchange rate. It is 1.2 million Kwanza to one U.S. dollar! Incredible!

In the afternoon, Barros shows up and we talk with him about helping us. He is ready. Before we go to meet the Minister of Religious Affairs, the five of us form a circle and have prayer. I feel the Lord's anointing as we hold hands. The Lord has a harvest of souls waiting for us in this country! The lady in the office tells us that tomorrow we must call on the Minister of Justice as well before she can give us the Certificate of Registration. This is as far as we could go today.

Jim's driver takes Barros, Romiro, and me to the Ministry of Religious Affairs to pick up a statement concerning registration with the Ministry of Justice. They do not have the document needed so we go directly to the Ministry of Justice itself and there we are given one. Before returning to the house, we have to pick up lined paper and revenue stamps. This takes some time to find. Finally, Jim is able to prepare the statement that asks a lot of questions. It is decided that Romiro, Barros, and Joao Antonio, plus the Dotys will be the national leaders of the church. By the time the statement is ready, it is too late to take it to them.

After breakfast, we again return to town with the driver. There are actually still some more things we must pick up and do before we can drop off the statement at the Ministry. When we do, we learn that they need another letter of information! So it is back to shopping for more of this specially lined paper that they require for official documents. Jim will again be busy on his computer this evening. When I check with the TAAG travel agent about my ticket, I am told that the flight is still fully booked! I am to return tomorrow. I mail Tiffany a postcard. Hopefully, she will get it.

We take the letters to the Notary for the stamp, seal, and signature. Then it is off to the Ministry of Justice. There we are told that the alphabets in front of the points listed on one of the letters are missing. Imagine! So we return to the house and Jim types them in. Then, it is back to the where we just came from. How many times is this now? Why are they making it so difficult for churches to be registered in this country?

When approaching the street corner, a large rat crawls out of an open sewer right where a policeman is standing! He jumps up with his legs spread apart and the rat scurries between them. A nearby pedestrian is openly shaken by what is taking place. It is difficult to know what it is that shocks her the most—the policeman doing the splits, or the frightened rat charging past her?

There are quite a few beggars on the streets of Luanda that have parts of their limbs missing. This is the result of land mines that they stumbled upon while working in their fields. One blind man comes up to our vehicle begging for money. The driver rolls down his window a portion and sticks some Kwanza through the crack. He reaches up and snatches it from his fingers! Now how did he know where the money was? Is he really blind?

I check about my ticket again and sit around until closing time. There is no room so I will be on standby in the morning. I am trusting in the Lord to get me on the plane, as there is plenty to do back in Zambia. All the paperwork is finally done for both ministries. The Certificate of Registration should be out in a week. I talk to

Ramiro and Barros tonight, along with the Dotys, about planting churches here in Angola.

Spend an hour in prayer this morning. I want the Lord to help me get on this morning's flight. The driver picks me up at 5:45 A.M. and drops me at the airport. I stand in a queue for an hour without getting anywhere. The place is packed with passengers waiting their turn to go somewhere. Finally, I ask for a seat in first class. One is left! No alternative but to take it, if I am to get home today. We board the plane at eight. Half an hour later it starts to taxi onto the runway and then stops. Mechanics show up and tinker around in the cockpit for an hour. Finally, we are ready to try again. Departure time is now an hour and a half late.

Half an hour into its flight, the plane turns and flies back to Luanda! No reason given, just some technical problems. We circle the city for some time before permission is granted for us to land. All of us disembark and begin waiting in the airport. When we finally are ushered back into the plane, it does not leave immediately. We sit in the plane for an hour before it decides to take off for Lusaka. It is now two o'clock. The flight has been delayed by six hours! The weather changes as we near Zambia. We run into rain. The whole time I was in Luanda there wasn't any.

Instead of 11:30 A.M., we land at 5:30 P.M. The case containing my clothes is not unloaded. The handlers go back several times to search the luggage section in the plane. It is finally found, thank the Lord! Mark and his two children are there to pick me up. We go on to Kirk's for supper. I finally end up at Avondale for the night. I call Marion at Livingstone to tell her that I am back, as she had called earlier to check on my whereabouts. She and those here at Avondale had been anxious about my delay.

*   *   *

On my next trip to Angola, Marion again stays behind at Livingstone. I am in Lusaka and catch a taxi to the airport. The plane lifts off for Luanda an hour and a half late. The flight is without mishap and when we arrive it takes half an hour before Air Zimbabwe is granted landing rights. It appears we missed our place in the queue for coming in late. No problem passing through Immigration. Jim Doty and his driver are present to meet me.

After dropping off my things at Doty's house, Dulci and the driver take me to see the site of the proposed church and school buildings at Viana, a township several kilometers east of Luanda. Jim Doty purchased the land and is donating a further amount to erect the buildings. Romiro, Jose Barros, and Joao Antonio are there. Joao knows quite a bit of English and helps to translate for me into Portuguese. After we return to the house, I visit with Jim.

I have a good night of rest. The Dotys are busy today, so I go alone to Viana with the driver. I meet with the three national leaders and we discuss the work until it is time to eat. Barros' wife prepares the meal. We are to meet again on Saturday. Dulci shows up in the afternoon for her classes with the youth.

While she has her meeting, I am taken to another compound where a congregation has been started. In Portuguese, the place is called Encouragement. This is where people who fled the civil war in the southeast were placed. About 120 have gathered to meet the missionary and to hear what the headman has to say. I am shown the site where a church and school is to be built. Presently they meet in a white building. The church leader says, "It's a real honor to have the missionary here in our midst. It's like a dream!" Before we leave, the headman serves me a cold drink at his house. We pick up Dulci and are back at their place by dark.

The driver shows up in the forenoon and I spend most of the day in town, as Jim and Dulci are both busy. The rate of exchange is now 5.5 million Kwanza to one U.S. dollar! That is the highest rate I have come across of any country in Africa, even higher than Zaire's worst days. The following day, Jim and I drop in at the Ministry of Justice and learn that the registration of the church is still pending! It was to have been done last month, but to-day we are told that it will now be next month. I check on my return flight at Air Zimbabwe. It is confirmed. This is so different from TAAG, the Angolan Airline. I answer Marion's e-mail tonight. Send one to Colleen as well.

Another hot and cloudless day! Jim is taking me to see the inside of the fort on the hill built many years ago by the Portuguese explorers. Its name, I believe, is Fort Sao Miguel. It is very spacious but does not have an interesting history as Fort Jesus does in Mombasa, Kenya. We also go out to see the slave museum, which is an hour's drive south of the city. There are a lot of baobab trees and villages scattered along the roadside. The museum is only a small building situated at the ocean's edge. I learn that four million slaves had been shipped by the Portuguese to labor in the fields of Brazil! On the return trip to Luanda, we stop at a roadside market where a lot of carvings are sold, especially in ivory.

In the morning we drive to Viana and it takes us an hour to get there. There are Sunday School classes before the main service. We are meeting under a canopy held up by poles. After a women's group sing their two songs and I am about to start my message, a strong gust of wind knocks over our shelter! The canvas and poles drop on top of us. Fortunately, no one is hurt. We all move inside one of the rooms as it begins to rain. There are over 100 of us crowded inside the building. I preach with Antonio translating and many ask for prayer. Several accept Christ as their Savior and others receive healing.

I meet with the three national leaders and the Dotys afterwards and we discuss the work here in Angola. I leave with them the first five books of the TEE program and the letterheads that I had made. Then we return to Luanda. The following day, Jim and Dulci are busy with their work so I am on my own. The driver takes me to town for a while and then I take it easy the rest of the day. I am returning to Lusaka tomorrow on my scheduled return flight.

I am up in time to eat breakfast with Jim and Dulci. Then the driver takes me to the airport. It takes some time to check through, but I make it. Thank the Lord! Not like last time. Almost everyone is smoking in the waiting room. Very humid as well, as the air conditioners are not working. Boarding takes some time as only one exit is being used even though there are two of them. The flight takes off an hour late and lands at Lusaka without any further delay. Mailes Ndao and Sarah Banda are there with a taxi to escort me back to Avondale. Mark could not make it. I phone Marion in Livingstone and she reports that all is well.

*   *   *

Before I can get my visa for Angola, it takes me literally weeks of running back and forth to their Embassy in Lusaka. This is the most difficult of all my previous trips. The day before I am to fly out, the Embassy needs a letter from Jim Doty stating that they will look after me during my stay in the country. I skip lunch and sit at the Embassy until the fax comes back from Jim in Luanda. My passport is finally stamped with a visa. It is now 3:30 P.M.! Unbelievable that it had to go beyond the wire, as the office hours here close at 3 P.M.!

In the morning I take a taxi to the airport. The Zambian Airways flight leaves at 9:30 A.M. for Harare. From there I fly on to Luanda on the Angolan Airliner TAAG. Three hours later I arrive and Jim is there waiting for me. We drive to Viana, where he picks up his wife. There has been great progress here at the plot! Classrooms have been erected and already 1,500 children are enrolled in school! I meet Joao Antonio and Jose Barros at the site. It is 5 P.M. before we arrive back at the house.

I prepare an Ordination Certificate in Portuguese this forenoon on Jim's computer. It will be presented to Barros on Sunday. In the afternoon, we drive out to Viana again. The two men, Barros and Antonio, are present, plus Romiro and a new man, Philip. There is a meeting with Antonio translating for me. Four laymen will be attending the nearby Nazarene Bible School for further training. We get back to the house by dark. Angola has changed their currency since my last visit. They dropped off six zeros from their old value. It is now twenty Kwanza to a U.S. dollar. The old one ended at 20 million (55 million on the streets)!

There are about one-hundred seventy people present for the Sunday morning service here at Viana. We are meeting in one of the larger classrooms. A church will be built in the near future here on the plot. There is singing with choir numbers before I conduct the ordination service for Jose Barros. I also preach the sermon afterwards. Joao Antonio is having trouble translating as he is suffering from malaria, so I shorten it. I give an altar call and many come forward. I pray for them without an interpreter.

There is food afterwards. Their staple food is not white maize as in Zambia, but yellow corn that they call *fufa*. I pray for Antonio that the Lord will touch his body. It is hot and humid, and finally it rains some after we get back to Doty's place. I meet the American missionary who is in charge of the Nazarene Bible School where our four men will be attending. I answer Marion's e-mail tonight on Jim's computer. Also send one off to Tiffany.

Both Jim and Dulci are busy today. Their driver is also tied up with other commitments, so I am housebound. It is impossible for me to move around when I do not have my own vehicle and do not speak Portuguese. I would like to travel into the interior and plant churches in the villages as I have done in other countries, but it is forbidden. Too dangerous!

I travel with Dulci and her driver to Viana where we met with the three national leaders. Discuss various aspects of the work, but the main topic is finances. Antonio is able to help me with the translation. It begins to rain and pours for at least half an hour. The school kids are just out for recess when it happens. They are running around in the rain enjoying every minute of it. Some roll around in the muddy water that is collecting in the low places. It is a real treat for them, as it does not rain here very often. It rains about five inches before it quits! Our meeting concludes at noon. After we eat, I visit with them until the driver shows up to take us back to the house. I work with Jim this evening on the *Constitution and By-laws* putting them into Portuguese.

Dulci is off to Viana this morning while Jim goes to his office. The driver takes me to check with TAAG about my return flight. I reconfirm it. No trouble with them this time. After a few more errands, we end up at the offices of Chevron where Jim works. I have lunch with him in their cafeteria. The driver drops me off at the house afterwards. It rains heavily this evening. Jose Barros is spending the night here and flying back to Cabinda tomorrow.

It is still raining this morning. Romiro drops in and eats breakfast with us. Joao Antonio has replaced him as the National Church Representative. He is still one of the national leaders but holding down another post. Jose is still the National Overseer. It just will not stop raining so we end up staying in doors all day.

I arise in the morning and prepare for my return flight. Jim is up before the driver comes for me at 5 A.M. We say our goodbye and I am off for the airport. There is no crowd today! Praise the Lord! I pass through Customs and Immigration quite easily. They do not even ask me if I have any of their local currency on me. The last time I had some and they took it from me.

I wanted so much to make one more trip to Angola, but I am unable to acquire a visa in time before my departure date from active service in Africa. I leave with one regret, that I could not fulfill my dreams for the work in Angola.

Zambia

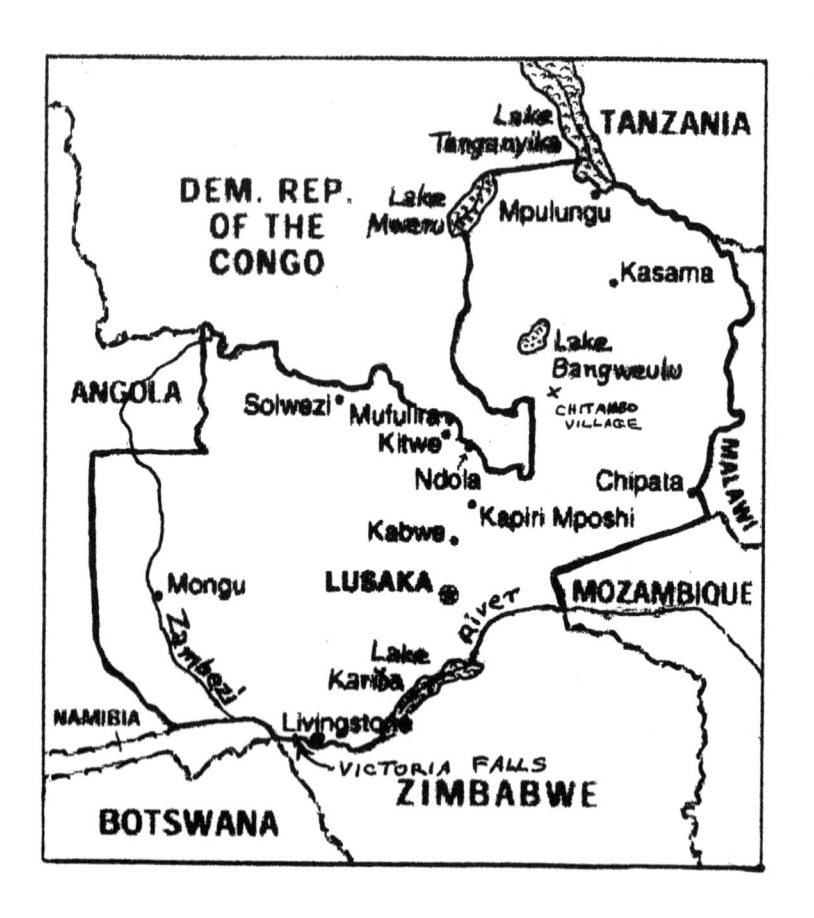

Thirteen
Pressing on in Zambia

There are now 424 churches with 47,500 members in Zambia as we enter the year 1996. We already have twenty-five districts where there are seven or more churches in each one of them. Truly the work of God has grown by leaps and bounds since our moving here mid 1989. Praise the Lord! There are still unreached areas though left in this country and so we press on with the Great Commission. The need for me to visit regularly the new works in Zimbabwe, Mozambique, and Malawi keeps me from traveling the districts in Zambia as often as I would like. Yet, I press on and as a result find myself on the move constantly. The Lord keeps renewing my strength, and my passion for the souls in Africa does not dim.

In this chapter, and in the following ones, I want to take you along to attend meetings that I will be holding in districts throughout Zambia. Most of them no longer are seminars lasting up to three days due to the lack of time on my part. Regional and district leaders now assist with the teaching program. Some of them are doing well, while others are not. Until men and women from abroad heed the call to come and assist me, this is the best I can do for Zambia.

First off, I will take you to Mongo District in Western

Province. On my previous journey there, I had given out many bags of maize, as there was a famine in the area. I had also made an effort to meet the Litunga, who is the Paramount Chief of the Lozi tribe. In fact, he calls himself the King of Barotseland, which takes in all of Western Province. I was not allowed to go straight to him but had to pass through the court first. Lungu, Musa, the District Chairman, and Ndalamei, the District Secretary, are with me. Everyone is required to kneel and clap before entering, but Lungu and I did not and we were excused because of being outsiders.

After explaining our mission, we were permitted to take the next step and that was to meet the minister. The same thing again: kneeling and clapping hands by everyone entering his presence. Here we were told that we could not see the Litunga because we did not bring along with us our *Constitution and Bylaws* plus our Registration. So that was that! The Litunga missed out receiving the gifts I had brought along for him. This place was like entering another country, a world of the past!

The evening before our journey, we attach the roof rack onto the Nissan Patrol and then load the used clothing onto it that Marion is sending along for the needy. The mattresses we put on top as well. The Bibles, TEE books, sleeping bags, and luggage we stick inside the vehicle. Gilbert Sommert, Joseph Jakobsh, and Ron Roesler who are visiting us from Canada are accompanying me on this trip. They arrived ten days ago and have already attended a service here in Lusaka at our church in Kanyama.

There they witnessed eight people set free from demon-possession. The demons had talked a lot. One that was refusing to leave said, "I have found a place which I will not leave." But finally the demon gave in and said, "I am tired of you all and I am leaving!" One man, who had several demons, had one that took a long time to cast out. It talked a lot, lying and trying to deceive us. In fact, it showed up while I was praying for the man after we thought all of them had been driven out! The Canadians had never seen anything like this before.

It is cool this morning when we get up. Ron has been very sick all night and cannot move this morning. So we lay hands on him and pray for his healing. The Lord answers and he gets right up out of bed. It's a miracle! He thought he would have to stay home but now he is going with us. Marion is remaining behind. We run into a lot of rough roads full of potholes. This is delaying our safari and we reach Ndiki Village in Mongo District at 4 P.M., later than usual. Six hundred people are waiting for us and they sing and dance as we enter the clearing where the services are to be held.

We go right into a worship service after all the greetings. Gilbert is the preacher. We pray for those who come up after the sermon. They seek salvation and healing. Nine are oppressed by demons and we drive them away in the name of Jesus. I never before saw so many with the same oppression. The demons were condemning them for being sick. Imagine?

We erect our tent before they serve us a meal of chicken and *nsima* made with maize and cassava. Then, we go into another service. I connect up the trouble light to the Nissan's battery and we have light. Jakobsh preaches and I say some words at the end. We pray for those who seek salvation afterwards. It is 9:30 P.M. when we retire into our tent. Two mattresses on the floor suffice all three of us to sleep comfortably. Ron has taken the day quite well. As for me I am somewhat tired from all the driving lately. Marion and I had taken the Canadians to see Victoria Falls, and Mosi oa Tunya Park a couple of days before this trip.

I am awake at four and do not go back to sleep. There are plenty of mosquitoes this morning. Before taking down the tent, I quickly shave with some of the water we brought along with us. Then I hand out the Bibles and TEE books to the pastors. No breakfast is served this morning. At 7:30, we are ready to hold the worship service. I am asked to bring the message. So I do. Many come forward for prayer. Then, communion is observed with many partaking. It takes some time before we are done.

The Canadians are given gifts, followed by speeches including one from the chief of the area. I give him a gift afterwards. Finally, we pass out the coats that Marion sent along. Many women miss out, as there are only thirty coats. It is midday when we leave for Lusaka. I again have to use the four-wheel drive to get through the ruts and the foot-deep fine dust before we reach the tarmac road. Once on it we come across trucks loaded with cattle for the slaughterhouse in Lusaka. I have trouble passing them because of the potholes everywhere on the road.

We also come across a five-foot Gaboon viper crossing the road in front of us. It is my first time to see one of these in the wild, and it is big! I stop for some pictures and while doing so the snake passes underneath the vehicle. Fortunately, it keeps going and does not crawl up a tire. We reach home by eight o'clock and are ready for the good supper that Marion has prepared.

*   *   *

Next, I will take you into North-Western Province. Up early, eat the breakfast Marion has prepared, pray for

His protection on my safari and for her at home, grab my case, crawl behind the wheel and drive out of the yard. The vehicle is full as we loaded all the Bibles, TEE books, songbooks, tracts, literature, used clothing, and sewing material for women into it last night. The road is rough all the way to Kaoma with very few patches where I can make any good time. In many places the tarmac is completely missing! I stop to eat the sandwiches that Marion has prepared for me while in Kafue National Park. Animals are around to keep me company, plus tsetse flies. The one I manage to kill is full of blood. Mine.

Ten kilometers beyond Kaoma, I take the short cut through the Black Forest and reach the pontoon that crosses the Kabompo River at two o'clock. Many Christians are waiting just across the river at the village of Watopa and I stop for a half an hour to listen to them sing for me. I carry on and at Mufuli Village the Christians again stop me. They sing for me as well. Finally, I reach Mumbeji where I pick up David Leyo and we drive on to Zambezi District for my first seminar in this province.

We arrive at 4 P.M. to a tumultuous welcome! They sing and dance as I drive up to their newly finished church near the town Zambezi. The iron sheets we helped them with are on the roof and it looks straight! After all the greetings, the choirs sing for us. Then, I bring the message. Many respond and come for prayer. Several hundred people are here for the weekend seminar. There is a district meeting that lasts till after dark. Eat something before checking in at the Council Guesthouse. President Chiluba is in town. He and his entourage are staying at the one I usually go to.

There is a lot of lightning and thunder tonight. The first I have seen and heard this year. I get settled just in time before the rain starts to fall. I use my sleeping bag to spread over the cot, as the bedding does not look clean. There is no screen on the window, so I use the net in the room and tuck it around me to keep away the mosquitoes. It is very hot in here. They provide me with a fan that I leave on all night. I sleep without a covering.

There is only one public bathroom, toilet, and sink in the guesthouse. I do not get a chance to shower and shave this morning as military men are bunked in the other rooms, and so the facilities are busy. I return to church at 7:30 A.M. and pass out some used clothing to the needy. Also, the tracts and magazines I brought along for the pastors. There is famine in some of the churches, so I will assist them with maize to be brought here for distribution to starving families.

The worship service starts at nine o'clock. The building is full. Robbell, the District Chairman, is given his First Course Certificate in the TEE program before we go into the communion service. Many partake of the bread and the cup. I bring the message and then take time to pray for all those who come for help. Most of them are sick and want healing. We eat after the service.

We say our goodbyes and rush off to Kakhoma Village in Chavuma District for our next meeting. People are waiting for us when we arrive and greet us with joyous singing! There are about 300 people present and we go into the service right away. Numerous songs are sung before I get a chance to share the Word of God. Many respond and come for help. I pray for the many who are sick. They just kept coming!

After the service, I give out used clothing to the needy. Two pastors are here from across the border in Angola, and they receive some as well. Also, pass out the tracts and magazines to the pastors, plus the patches of material to the women. I am given several gifts, including a goat from Robbell that I cannot take with me on this trip. When then? I am always full and on my way to the next place!

It is already dark when I drive to the town Chavuma to book into the guesthouse there. It has no running water and no power! There is a candle in the room but I refrain from using it much, as insects are plentiful. It is raining with plenty of lightning and thunder so I skip going to the river for a dip. Another hot night! I lower the mosquito net from the ceiling and then try to keep curled up inside it so the mosquitoes cannot reach me. My bed is like a hammock!

In the morning I march down to the Zambezi River and have a good wash. It is my first in a couple of days. Also shave off my beard of two days. Feel much better now, as I did a lot of sweating the last two nights due to the high humidity. There are others who are also taking a bath in the river. The Chavuma Falls is right nearby. More like rapids, as they are very small. Eat some of the lunch that I still have left over from home before I return to Kakhoma Village for the service.

I am also helping four churches in this district with famine relief. The two pastors from Angola are given a bag of maize as well. After the singing and my message, many accept Christ as their Savior. Some have also come for healing. We observe the Lord's Supper in which I handle the cup. Many elderly and aged participate. I notice their weatherworn faces, from years spent toiling under the hot African sun. I am touched and fight back the tears. It is a service I will never forget! Before we leave, I receive several gifts as I did at Zambezi.

We reach Mumbeji in Kabompo District at 3 P.M. The service promptly starts and, before long, I am delivering the message. Most of those present come for prayer. We have special prayer for the very sick. There are five who are demon-possessed. One of those is a woman who has seven demons; one of them is a mad spirit! Another one, a man, has two traditional spirits. Even a little old woman has two, as well, so strong that they toss us about! Another woman has a demon in her legs. My first time to see this! They keep jerking her knees.

It takes us some time to cast out all the demons from the five people. Most of them were quite powerful and we had all to do to handle them! I am all wet with perspiration and when they have prepared my water, I take a bath in the outdoor enclosure. The women prepare us food and, after I have eaten, I prepare my bed for the night in one of the huts. I throw my foam mattress on the floor and then crawl inside the sleeping bag for some shut-eye.

I have a good night in spite of a rude awakening at 9:30 last night by loud drums and lively singing! For a while I didn't know where I was because of coming out of a deep, deep sleep. I was trying to figure out where I was? They were the youth choirs practicing. This morning I pass out the tracts, magazines, sewing patches, and used clothing. Leave some of the things with Leyo for the ones in Angola who have not come today. He will be going there in the near future.

At church, I preach in the main service and then pray for many afterwards. We also hold a Communion service followed by a choir contest. I am asked to be one of the judges. Their singing needs improving. Young people sing all day long, and all night if we would allow it, but it is mostly repetitious. There is food afterwards. Then we leave for Manyinga, also in Kabompo District, for our next service. Kakinga, the district chairman, is coming with Leyo and me. His bicycle is on top of the roof rack.

We reach Manyinga at 3 P.M. People are waiting at

the church, more than we had at Mumbeji. It is very hot inside as the building is full. I preach and the Lord again anoints and many come for prayer. Also pray for the sick and for two who are oppressed by demons in their dreams. After the service, there is a meeting. It is dark when we quit. Water is brought for my bath and I have one before we eat. The meat they serve is from a duiker. I am sleeping tonight in their storeroom. It looks like rain so I am not setting up my tent.

As it turns out it only sprinkled a couple of times during the night. I used the net to keep away the mosquitoes and other insects so I slept well. I have a bath and shave before we eat. Give out the stuff for this place as we did at the other places. We assemble in church at eight. After the choirs sing there is a child dedication service where I pray for six of them. In the main worship service, the Lord anoints the message and the whole congregation drops to its knees for prayer! The Holy Spirit is moving in their midst. I am given a gift before we leave for Mwinilunga District.

The road from Manyinga to Mwinilunga starts off fine as they are starting to repair it, but when we reach the old stretch we slow down considerably. There are bad washouts from all the rain they have been having. The bridge that we found washed away on my last safari, I now find has been repaired. It is past noon when we reach Mwinilunga. John Kapimbi, the district chairman, is waiting for us. Fill up with diesel and continue on to Katuyola Village where the district convention is to be held.

The service starts as soon as we arrive. There is no church building here so we meet outside. After all the songs, I preach and many come forward. The Lord has been blessing the messages throughout this trip. There is a district meeting afterwards that gets interrupted by rain. There is plenty of lightning and thunder. When it stops, we conclude our business meeting. We just get through eating a good meal when the rain returns. Lots of rain comes down with dangerously close lightning! Some marble-sized hail falls as well. I take refuge in the vehicle. Finally, it lets off at nine and I am taken to spend the night in the vice chairman's house.

I have a candle lit all night so as to keep the rats at bay! I see them on the walls above me, their eyes staring down at me. It is a restless night, as the rain is leaking through in several places from the ceiling. My two-inch foam mattress I am using needs to be thicker as it is not comfortable this time. All is wet in the morning, but it soon begins to dry when the sun comes out. Breakfast is delayed because of the rainy night.

By the time the main service starts, I have given out the tracts, magazines, used clothing, and the patches of material for the women. We pray for the District Committee and observe the Lord's Supper before I deliver the sermon. It is a tough message and nearly all come for prayer. There is one oppressed and twelve possessed people who want to be delivered. Most of them have seven or more demons! One girl has twelve of them. Many of the demons are ancestral and traditional. A couple of them have mad spirits. One demon in a woman gets very violent. Leyo almost gets hit twice when she takes a swipe at him!

I am wringing wet, and so is Leyo, from the strenuous work of driving out the demons. It takes three hours to cast them all out! I am exhausted by the time it is done which is 2 P.M., the time we were to have been in Solwezi! There was one girl who kept crying and would not say anything except to scream once in a while. She took some time. Quite a few from the choir were possessed. I knew already yesterday that one of the girls was possessed. Her facial expressions told me that she was. I am discovering that many young people in the choirs throughout Zambia are not saved.

We eat before leaving for Solwezi District. The women serve us caterpillars along with some other dishes. They are the stripped ones that eventually turn into butterflies. It's a great feast! It is almost five o'clock when we arrive at the church in Solwezi town. The Lord renews my strength and I am able to preach in the service. The whole congregation comes for prayer! Praise the Lord! The women serve all the leaders, including myself, food at the church. There is a district meeting afterwards. It gets quite hot at times when it comes to discussing the district chairman. It is after 8 P.M. when I turn in at the motel here in town.

I do not have a full night of sleep, too many concerns for the work keep running around in my head. Back at church by 7:30 A.M. and distribute the stuff before eating with the leaders. In the service I give the Vice Chairman his First Course Certificate in the TEE program. Then we observe the Lord's Supper before I preach in the worship service. Many come for prayer again after my message. Two of them complain of sickness, but it turns out they have demons! This makes it more difficult to drive them out since they have not confessed to having them and wanting to be rid of them. The one, who finally admits having a demon, goes readily when we command it to leave.

But the demon in the second woman keeps refusing to leave. This young woman sings in the choir and I knew last night when she sang that she has a demon! The demon in her keeps talking to us, calling us dogs and for us to leave her alone. It is very strong as well and tosses us around. At one juncture, I am knocked back on my haunches! By my pure stubbornness and perseverance, the demon is finally driven out in the name of Jesus! In all there were three possessed and one oppressed who were delivered.

It is noon when the service ends. I immediately leave for Lusaka and home. No problem along the way and arrive at 6 P.M., wrapping up 2,155 kilometers on this trip. All is fine here. Marion has prepared a nice meal. It is delicious! It beats anything I ate on my ten-day safari, and that includes the caterpillars.

Fourteen
Engaged Further Afield

Today, I am traveling to Luangwa District in Central Province. Marion is coming along, as well as Mailes, Tembo, and Moyo. The Great East Road has many potholes. This slows us down considerably. When we reach the Luangwa Bridge, we turn off onto a gravelled road and drive south for 85 kilometers until we reach the Luangwa boma (district offices), once called Feira during the colonial days. It is built at the concourse of two rivers, the Luangwa and the Zambezi. The town of Zumbo lies east just across the river in Mozambique.

We discover that Elliott, the district chairman, has not booked us into any guesthouse, so we are without a bed tonight! There is room tomorrow though at one place. We drive down to where the Luangwa River flows into the Zambezi. Quite a view! It is so nice and peaceful. A good thing Marion has brought along a lunch and we eat it now. Those with us are happy that Marion is along. They are talking among themselves that when Bwana travels without Mama, he does not stop for anything to eat along the way!

We as yet do not have a church building here so the believers meet at the school. There are about 200 crowded into the classroom for the evening service. Some Mozambican Christians have come from across the

Luangwa River to attend the service, as well as Zimbabwean Christians from across the Zambezi River. It is quite a meeting of believers from three different countries brought together in Christ! There is much rejoicing. Moyo shares from the Word before we conclude the service.

After we disperse, Marion and I bed down in the Nissan Patrol. She takes the middle seats and I am on the front ones. Mailes is sleeping in Elliott's hut, while Moyo and Tembo are in one of the classrooms. We turn in without a bath. It is a hot night, so we cannot close the windows all the way. Mosquitoes are coming inside and bothering us. Hopefully, we will not come down with malaria. I sure do not want another bout so soon after my last one three weeks ago. I had the chills so bad that it shook the whole bed! It racked my body for half an hour. Then, I had temperatures of 103, off and on, for a couple of days. Ended up having to take a course of quinine tablets to get rid of the malaria.

We wake up to a nice day here in the valley. It looks like another hot day. Mailes has breakfast with us at the guesthouse we will be staying in tonight. At nine o'clock, we meet in the classroom for our worship service. After the choirs and specials, I bring the message. Many come forward for salvation and for healing. There are four oppressed by demons. We pray for them and for the one who also has deafness in her ear. There are two demon-possessed who need deliverance. One has four demons and the other one has three of them. I am soaked with perspiration when all the demons have finally been driven out.

They feed the five of us in a nearby house. Then we return to the school and I meet with the local congregation while Marion and Mailes teach the group from Mozambique. The Zimbabweans left right after dinner. We had prayer with them before their departure. In the evening, the Mozambicans return to their homes across the river. Tembo then leaves to hold a service at one of our churches up the road. Marion and I, along with Mailes, book into one of the guesthouses. Moyo finds a room at the Council Rest House. We visit for a while and after we eat supper, we turn in for the night.

Mosquitoes bother Marion throughout the night, as she did not have a net over her bed. I had one with holes in it but I do not believe any got inside it. Moyo and Elliott show up for breakfast and eat with us. When done, we start out for Lusaka. When we reach the shops at Luangwa Bridge, I buy 40 liters of diesel from someone selling it from a jerry can. This should take us home. They did not have any at the Luangwa boma. Marion buys a bunch of fresh fish for us and everyone else. They are tied onto the roof rack. We arrive home mid afternoon.

*   *   *

Another trip to Western Province worth mentioning is the one where Warren Senft from Alberta, Canada is traveling with me. He has come to assist the work for five weeks. He has already been to Eastern Province escorted by Moyo, as I was laid up with a fractured rib. I now am recuperated sufficiently to make this trip. The bundles of used clothing have already been loaded onto the roof rack, plus all the materials I always take with me are packed inside the vehicle. Mailes and Moyo are coming on this trip as well. Their luggage goes up on top. Marion is not coming.

It is eight o'clock when we leave the yard for Kaoma District. The road is rough all the way from Lusaka to

Kafue National Park. But it is okay through the park where we see some game, and then on to the town of Kaoma. Here we meet Musa at the filling station. He said there is no food at the village we are going to so I buy some to take along. We buy a soda and eat the sandwiches that I brought along. Then we drive one hundred kilometers beyond Kaoma before turning off into the sandy bush-covered countryside. It is slow going even in four-wheel drive, branches scraping both sides of the vehicle. Only for the gospel's sake will one do it!

Two hours and 47 kilometers later, we spot the place we are going to for our seminar. It is beyond a stream that we cross without a problem. The villagers give us a warm welcome and feed us an hour later. The meal consists of chicken and rice with some greens and *nsima*. It is dark by now. There is still a service with songs and a sermon from Moyo. Several request prayer. It is after ten when I retire into my small tent. Warren and Moyo are sleeping in the big one while Mailes is bunking down with the women inside the church building.

I wake up to the chirping of tree frogs. A dove soon joins in with its cooing. We are given the same menu as last night for our breakfast. Afterwards Mailes gives out the used clothing to the ones who need them most, plus the sewing material to the women. Then we go into the worship service with Warren preaching the sermon. We pray for those who come forward, including two who are oppressed by demons. There is also a woman from whom we cast out a demon that had possessed her for years.

After dinner we divide into three groups. Mailes takes the women, Moyo and I meet with the district committee, and Warren takes the rest of the men. The committee is revamped. Too many officers come from one congregation, so we spread them out to include other churches. In the evening, we hold our last service of the day. I preach this time. There is freedom and the Lord blesses the message. Again, one demon-possessed person is dealt with and two of them are cast out of her.

We eat our supper after dark. A candle serves as a light. Finally, there is a time for choruses and testimonies beside a roaring campfire. Several share and Mailes closes the meeting with the story of her conversion. It was a nice time of fellowship, ending at 11 P.M.! Turn into my tent with a runny nose, due to the dust around here. I had trouble with it, especially inside the church building.

I get up at six o'clock. Actually, I was awake earlier because of those who were talking and praying beside the campfire. We take down the tents and load them and our stuff onto the roof rack. Then we have tea and some fritters that Mailes made for our breakfast. It is eight when we say goodbye and leave for our next seminar. We take a different route back to the tarmac road than the one we came in on. This one is much shorter and not as rough on the vehicle.

We reach Ndiki Village in Mongo District at eleven o'clock. After a cup of tea and some bananas, we go into the service. Warren delivers the message. There are those who respond and come for prayer, including an oppressed woman and another one who is possessed. We cast out the demon from her. Afterwards I have a district meeting while Mailes meets with the women and Warren teaches those who are not in any of the other two groups. I do some teaching as well with my group. After the meetings, we finally get our first real meal at 5 P.M.

Before the service starts tonight, I take a well-deserved shower. We are meeting beside the campfire. Moyo brings the sermon and we pray for many afterwards. During the closing prayer, the Lord anoints me and reveals to me that there is a serious problem here in this district. The crowd is much smaller from my last visit. Sure enough, when I confront Musa, I learn that he has taken a new wife into his house after his other one divorced him. There was no church wedding performed, which as a district leader he should have done. We are all shocked! He will have to give an account to the Executive Committee when we meet later this month.

It was cold here last night. We pack up our tents and all our bedding onto the vehicle before breakfast. While eating, some chicken meat gets stuck in my throat and I have trouble dislodging it. I can hardly breathe and nudge Warren to slap me on my back. He reaches over and does just that, which helps to jar the wad of meat loose. This is the first time this sort of thing has happened to me! Mailes and Moyo sat stunned through it all, not knowing what to do. I need to chew the meat of these tough chickens they have here into smaller pieces before swallowing. Finally, Mailes exclaims, "It was Satan trying to get rid of you!" Was it?

I preach in the worship service and the Lord anoints the message, the most for some time. I am touched by it myself. This time we take time to pray for each one separately that comes forward. It is eleven o'clock when we get done. We are given gifts of cowhide-covered stools and woven baskets before we can start our journey back to Lusaka. The trip goes well and we make good time. It takes us only seven hours to reach home. We clocked 1,225 kilometers on this trip.

*   *   *

Another trip to the North-Western Province that bears mentioning is the following one. Oscar and Mailes

Ndao are along with me, plus Helga Stalts who has come from Alberta, Canada for two months. Marion is staying to direct the container onto our yard that was shipped from the States some time ago.

I need to say that Helga, the day she arrives, finds herself in a women's seminar here in Lusaka. She teaches in one of the classes the following day. She is present in the Sunday service where 170 are present. There is lots of singing. After my message one of those who come for prayer is demon-possessed. She has a mad demon that is very strong and thrashes about violently! There is a grin on the woman's face and she claws at her bosom. It takes us ten minutes to drive out the demon. After her deliverance, the woman looks inside the top of her dress to see where the demon had gone! Kirk's girls, Ashling, Shaina, and Mikaela are present and they enjoyed the whole service.

As I already have mentioned, Helga is with us on this trip. After crossing the Kabompo River on the pontoon, we stop at Mufuli Village where we have a makeshift dispensary and a church. Many people have gathered for the convention and we are greeted warmly. They have erected enclosures out of reeds for eating and sleeping quarters. The latrines and showers are made out of the same material. We set up our tents. I am using the small one while Helga and Mailes are using the larger one. Oscar is sleeping with the Chairman in one of the enclosures.

I use the trouble light, clipped to the vehicle battery, for the service tonight. I preach and many come for prayer. A couple of plays by the youth afterwards take us till 11 P.M. before we can retire for the night. Up at six, as the camp is alive by then. Oscar and Helga start treating patients right after breakfast. Mailes talks to the women and gives them their sewing material that Marion sent along. I interview applicants for orphan assistance and accept five new ones. I give two orphans who were accepted earlier their allowance for this quarter.

Over 150 sick were waiting to be treated but there is not enough time to do them all. Oscar and Helga are able do about one third of them and then we must move on to our next destination, as it is already ten o'clock. They give us several gifts before we leave.

There is a big welcome for us when we arrive at the church near Zambezi town. After all the speeches and greetings, we are given something to eat. Then Oscar and Helga speak on health and diseases before we break into classes. In the evening there is a worship service and I deliver the message after all their specials. The Lord blesses! Very many come for prayer; one of those has epileptic fits while another one has eight demons. It takes some time, but finally they all leave the woman.

After supper we check into the Zambezi Motel for the night. We all are dehydrated and immediately down several cold soft drinks. Mailes and Helga are in one room while Oscar and Leyo are in theirs. There is hot water so I have a nice shower. It is stuffy and hot in my room, so I keep the window open even though there is no screen. To keep away the mosquitoes, I leave the fan on all night.

After a fairly good night, we all meet at the church again. I interview the orphans and their guardians, and then accept a couple new ones. Speak with the seventeen Angolans that have come from across the border to see me. They walked four days to get here. They inform me that there are now five churches in Mukando District. These are different from the five that are across the border from Chavuma where I had gone one day for a service. I told them I would be registering the Church of God in

Angola as soon as I get to the capitol Luanda. Oscar and Helga have been treating the sick during all this time. They give us many gifts before we leave.

The Christians welcome us with songs and speeches when we arrive at Kakhoma, the central church in Chavuma District. I see no aftermath of the clashes that took place here in Chavuma District between the Lunda and Luvale tribes. Apparently nine died after drinking some *mowa* (homemade brew) at a wedding. The Lunda are accusing the Luvale and several have died and many houses burned as a result. There has been no love between the two tribes since way back when their first chiefs argued and fought over where the boundaries should be.

Before they serve us food, Oscar and Helga share on health. Then I interview the orphans and give them their allotment. Accept a couple more applicants for sponsorship. We break into classes so that we all can teach. I preach in the evening service and then we pray for those who come forward. Before it gets dark, we erect our tents beside the church. There will be no privacy for us tonight! Mailes brings the message in the service after supper. My trouble light comes in handy again. It is 11 P.M. before we can get to bed.

This morning while I am packing up, Oscar and Helga treat the sick that have come. After breakfast we say our farewells, and they present us with many gifts, one being a guinea fowl. I like their music here, especially their drums which are mellow and not so loud. Also, enjoyed hearing their youth and women choirs.

At Zambezi we stop at the district chairman's house to pick up the three chickens given as gifts yesterday. His wife invites us to help eat one of them that she has cooked! The other two hens we stick in a woven cage along with the guinea fowl, and tie it to the roof rack. When we reach Manyinga, we discover one of the chickens is missing! It had gotten out and is somewhere in the bushes right now. A hawk will surely find it.

After the greetings, we eat again. Then we break into classes. In the evening we have the worship service. As usual choirs sing before I get to preach. The Lord anoints the message. Very many come forward, including those possessed with demons. While casting out one from a woman, another demon manifests itself in someone else. At one time we have three different women manifesting demons! Most of the demons keep screaming, making it difficult to cast them out quickly. One demon speaks up in a woman that is still seated in the audience, "I told you we should not have come!" It is speaking to the one we are in the process of casting out. Where is Helga? She is top of a bench trying hard to stay out of the way of all the activity.

When we are dealing with another person, blood begins to ooze from her mouth and nose! It is none of our doing but Satan's. We continue to command the demon to leave. As it goes, the bleeding miraculously stops! When it is too dark inside the church, we move outside to continue setting captives free. The headlights of the vehicle are used. In all there are nine people who are finally delivered from demonic possession. One had twenty, others ten, nine, seven, and so on. Most of the women are choir members! I am all wet when it is over. Mailes shares after supper in an outdoor service.

At 2:45 A.M., a man stumbles past my tent muttering, "There are fourteen apostles not twelve." "It is not good what you are doing." "This is not a bicycle, it is an automobile." The rest of his conversation is in the Luvale language. In the morning when I relate last night's events, Mailes and Helga report that they did not hear the drunk.

Take two applications for the orphan program before breakfast. Also, the giving of gifts is done before we eat. Finally we say our farewells and drive off. A good ending!

An hour later we arrive at a church in Mfumbwe District where Christians have met to receive us. We disperse into classes for an hour before assembling in a worship service. I share and several want prayer afterwards. One of them is a man who was bitten by a dog two weeks ago. Register a couple of orphans before leaving. A short visit but helpful, I believe, to this new district.

We take the short cut to Mwinilunga from Manyinga. Helga drives for a while. When we reach Mwinilunga, a crowd of Christians meet us as we enter town and escort us all the way through it until we reach the church. They are dancing and singing all around the vehicle! I have to drive slowly so as not to run into them. It is the biggest welcome thus far in Zambia!

After the welcome speeches, we eat and then I call Marion from a phone in town. She wanted to know whether we arrived safely. Mikaela, our granddaughter, is with her. Mailes preaches in the evening service. We are gathered outside, as the church is too small. I use the trouble light again. It is late when we check into the guesthouse. It has been a full day!

In the morning, we return to church and the women serve us breakfast. Then Mailes gives out the women's material and Oscar with Helga share about health. Afterwards I preach and the Lord anoints the message and me! Many come forward for salvation and healing. There are three demon-possessed who seek deliverance. The two women and a man keep on trembling until the demons are driven out of them. One woman has only one while the younger one has eleven demons! It takes us a while to cast them out of her. This delays our departure from Mwinilunga.

The meal they serve us before we leave includes caterpillars. We all take some except for Helga. I can't persuade her to eat even one. It is already 5 P.M. when we finally arrive three hours late at the church in Solwezi. There are some people still waiting for us, while others have gone home. We immediately have a service and many respond to my message. The women's district leader takes us to her home for supper. After we eat Mailes speaks tonight in yet another service. It is 10 P.M. when we turn in at the motel.

We return to church and the women serve us breakfast. Then Mailes passes out the used clothing to the women while I register the three orphans that are brought to me. I am given a chicken. The guinea fowl had to be butchered yesterday, as it was about to die. Only the rooster is left now, plus the chicken just given me. We say our farewells and leave at ten o'clock for Lusaka.

While I take a nap, Helga again relieves me for a spell at the wheel. I wake up abruptly when I hear a horn blaring and Helga saying, "Why don't they get out of the way?" She does not recognize them to be policemen manning a roadblock and uses the horn once again! By now I am wide-awake and manage to get her to stop just in time. Needless to say, the officer is not too happy with us. We reach home safely without a further incident. During our seven days' absence, Marion has done a lot of unpacking and repacking in the container that just arrived. I am too tired to look at the stuff. Tomorrow is another day.

Fifteen
Always So Much to Do

The day before my next planned trip, this time to Luangwa District, I come down with malaria in the morning. I have chills all forenoon. Then at noon fever sets in. It lasts until bedtime. I use a cloth dipped in cold water but still the fever does not break. It hangs around 103 to 104 degrees. I take Halfan at nine, then at three, and finally at nine tonight. I begin sweating soon afterwards. It is a relief that the fever has finally broken. Marion is not here. She went to Livingstone with Mark and his family.

The bedding is all wet this morning. Even the towels are that I kept replacing on top of my pillow are soaked. I really did a lot of sweating! I feel weak but otherwise okay. I am well enough to make the trip to Luangwa. Don Riley, the new Regional Director for Africa, and his wife Paula who are here visiting will be traveling with me today. So are Helga, who is still with us, plus Oscar and Chitui of Mozambique. We leave Lusaka right after breakfast.

Helga drives the Nissan as far as Rufunsa, then Don takes over for the rest of the way. We arrive at noon and book in at the guesthouse. We find Tembo already here. He came earlier by minibus. Then I take them to the river where the Luangwa empties into the Zambezi. It is a grand sight! We pull ourselves away and gather at the same school where we were last time. They serve us food under the nearby baobab tree before we have our service. Oscar preaches the message after all their songs are sung. When we finish dealing with those who come forward, we return to the river and enjoy the cool breeze. I spot a crocodile in the Zambezi.

After a supper of chicken and rice, we return for another service. Don preaches this time. Two of those that come forward are demon-possessed. It takes a while to drive them all out. Rileys and Helga assist me with the first one, and then Oscar and Tembo help me with the second one. I am sweating a lot during this time. It is late before we are done. When I check into my room, I come down with a very high fever. There is no warm water in the taps, so I use cold water to sponge myself off before crawling into bed.

I do a lot of sweating during the night. All the bedding gets wet. I feel better for it, though, this morning. I need to as I am preaching this forenoon. While sitting on a lawn chair in front of the guesthouse, quietly waiting for the rest to show up, a bird flies by and leaves its calling card on my head and collar! Helga discovers it when she shows up. Until then, I am unaware of it. "Birds sing for other people!"

When we arrive at the school, we are given tea and buns. I hand out the Bibles, songbooks, and tracts we brought along. Each side gets their share—Mozambique, Zimbabwe, and Zambia. Then we start the service. There is plenty of singing before I deliver my message. I find it easy preaching, as they are an attentive audience, amening and clapping their hands a lot. Many come to the front. We pray for the sick and those who seek forgiveness, plus for the one who is oppressed by evil spirits. The service ends at high noon. It is another hot day!

I am helping with famine relief, as there is drought here in the valley. Some of the maize is going to Mozambique and Zimbabwe as well. I register an orphan for the Kinderhilfswerk program and pass out a crutch to a lame girl. We then drive the 85 kilometers to the Great East Road. Here at the shops I purchase 20 liters of diesel for the vehicle from a vendor. When we arrive home, Marion is waiting for us. We visit until 10:30 P.M., a bit late for me.

Before Helga leaves us for Canada, she attends the worship service here at Avondale that lasts three and a half hours! We have 250 worshippers present and it gets very hot inside the building. There is a full program with many specials and choirs. Marion and Helga sing a duet. Graduates in the TEE program receive their certificates and recognized ministers their licenses. We also pray for the regional and national leaders. My message "Steadfastness" touches the leaders and many of them come forward for prayer.

*   *   *

This trip will take us to Luapula and Northern Province. We load up the Nissan Patrol in the evening. Marion is taking along lots of used clothing that we stack on the roof rack. The Bibles, songbooks, TEE books, tracts, Sunday School material, and camping equipment such as the mattress, sleeping bag, and tent, go in back of the vehicle. Our suitcase, brief case, and lunch will be put inside when we leave in the morning.

It is 7:30 A.M. when we leave the yard. Mailes is traveling with us this time. At Kapiri Mposhi, I stop to fill up with diesel and kerosene. I have learned that mixing both together gives a better performance. Today there is none of either at the pumps. There has been a shortage of fuel in Lusaka as well. I make it to Mkushi and find some there, so I fill up the vehicle. It is taking more fuel today than normal, probably due to the high load on top. At noon we stop beside the road and eat the lunch Marion has brought along.

We cross the long bridge across the Luapula River. It is more like a causeway as it is two miles long. Turn in at Samfya to fill up and find no diesel or kerosene at the only pump in town. Someone comes with us and directs us to places that may have fuel. But we strike out; even the police and WWF (World Wildlife Federation) do not have a drop to spare! Finally, we end up at the mission station that sits right on the shores of Lake Bangweula. The missionary spares us five liters of kerosene that we pour into the tank. That should take us now to Mansa, our destination. But we are told that there is no diesel there, in fact there is none to be had in all of Luapula Province! Well, we are still trusting in the Lord that He will provide. He has brought us thus far. He will not fail us now!

Twenty kilometers this side of Mansa, we stop at Mabumba Village where we will be holding our seminar. Tyson the regional leader is waiting for us. It is now 5 P.M. At dark, we hold a service outside the house we will be sleeping in. The owner is Lovemore Chanda, a teacher at a school here in the village. It is late before we can retire for the night.

We had a reasonable good night on the floor. Marion was awake more than me, as she had a lone mosquito pestering her. She also heard a bat flying about and a rat jump from the wall. I did see a large cockroach crawling on the floor in front of me. A rooster, just outside our window, wakes us up before dawn. I take a bath in a grass enclosure before breakfast. The latrine is low and made out of bricks with a grass roof. As I enter it, there is a sharp turn to my left that I have difficulty maneuvering. It is awkward for me to get in and out!

I rush to Mansa early to check for diesel. Tyson and Lovemore come along. The diesel tanker has just pulled in and I am able to fill the Nissan, plus the two twenty-liter containers that I buy from a peddler. So I am okay now. Buy some maize and a few other things for the seminar before heading back. I find Marion and Mailes teaching a class for both women and men. Tyson takes me to see the chief at his palace nearby. I am expected to do this. When I do not kneel, he tells me it is customary to do so. Therefore, I oblige and clap my hands at the same time as a sign of respect. After chatting for a while, his wife brings a chicken and tomatoes that he hands over to me. I then give him a Bible, a songbook, and some money as my gift to him. We then leave.

It is my turn to teach a class for the men and women. We break for dinner and then reassemble again. This time Marion and Mailes meet with the women while I have the men that include pastors. We quit shortly after 4 P.M. Marion then passes out the used clothing. When she is done, I give out Bibles and songbooks, plus literature for the youth and women. Marion signs up six new orphans for Kinderhilfswerk. It is now dark. After supper we talk a while and call it quits for the night at nine o'clock.

Cockroaches bother us during the night. Marion kills more than thirty of them with insect spray and her shoe! They crawl over our sleeping bag and even inside it, as we can't zip up totally due to the heat. The worship service starts right after breakfast in one of the classrooms at a school. We have 120 attending and many want prayer after my sermon. Before closing the service, we observe the

Lord's Supper. We leave for Mporokoso District at ten o'clock.

At the Kalungwisha River that separates Luapula and Northern Provinces, we turn off the road and travel nine kilometers into the bush to see the Lumangwa Falls. It is beautiful! Not like Victoria Falls but magnificent just the same. We have the scones and drinks at this time that Marion bought on our way through Mansa town. It is 4 P.M. when we reach Shamwamba Village near the town of Mporokoso, the place where we are to hold our seminar.

We go into the service immediately. The little church is full with many more crowded outside the building. There are 300 people present. I preach and many seek repentance after the message. The children began to be quite noisy during the end of my message, so I took time to reprimand them and the parents. I told them they were in the house of God! After the service the choirs sing for us outside. Then we walk to meet the chief, as he had asked that we come. I had met him two years earlier. I take Marion, Mailes, and Tyson with me. It is a nice visit. The chief gives us a plot of ground near the river for our central church here in Mporokoso District.

Mailes preaches tonight after Marion gives the children a story. It is a good meeting with many requesting prayer. Afterwards, Tyson and Mailes lead in some choruses outside. I put up the trouble light. Marion and I are sleeping tonight in a small room next to where the women are sleeping. Numerous rats are scurrying around in the next room because of the food that is being stored there. They do not disturb us, except for the noise.

They bring us water for bathing to our room this morning. After Marion and I are done, breakfast is waiting. It has been *nsima* every meal with rice for breakfast at times. The meat when served is chicken, with an exception last night when it was duiker. After we eat, Marion passes out used clothing to the poorest of the poor. Then it is time for our classes. Marion and Mailes take the women and I have the men. I am asked many questions especially on polygamy and divorce. We quit at 10:30 A.M.

It is now time for the communion service. I share from the Word before we observe it. It is one of the best services on the Lord's Supper we have had for some time because the Spirit of the Lord was so present! I was really touched.

We leave at noon for Nasama Village in Kaputa District after filling up with diesel. It's very expensive here! The people are waiting for us when we arrive at the church. The worship service starts right away. The Lord blesses the message and many seek Him for salvation and healing. A woman, who for some time now has been going deaf, is brought for healing. People have to shout when talking to her. When we start praying for her, a demon manifests itself! It isn't long and she is delivered, and able to hear normally again. God is great!

There are five individuals who are possessed with demons. Most of them have traditional and ancestral spirits but a couple of them also have snake demons. One even has a leopard demon, my first! The last one to be delivered has demons that are very strong and keep refusing to vacate. But ultimately they do leave. I do not give up! I take charms off six babies who are brought up for prayer. It is after 4 P.M. when the service ends.

Marion and I set up our tent before going to eat. Instead of it being dinner it is our supper. All of us are weak from missing the noonday meal and wrestling with demons! Afterwards Marion takes applications for six orphans. Then we hold a service outside with many choruses before Mailes gives her story and I preach. She translates for me. The youth present a play on the crucifixion after the close of the service. Another full day! It is good to sleep in the tent tonight as it gives us some privacy.

Before breakfast, we take down the tent. Then Marion with Mailes give out the used clothing, while I pass out the Bibles and songbooks. After we eat, I go to see the chief as he requested my presence. But he is away, so I return to the church. While I teach the men, Marion and Mailes teach the women. Marion discovers the women are very steeped in traditional beliefs. There is yet so much darkness among the Zambian women.

We all gather in the church and observe the Lord's Supper. After the service, we pack up to depart for Kasama District. It is difficult to leave, as they want to feed us first. I refuse as otherwise we will be late for the next service. We are given gifts of bananas, two chickens, rice, and baskets. It is 2 P.M. when we reach the place of our next seminar, a short distance from the town of Kasama.

The service starts right after we have something to eat. I preach and six of those we deal with are people oppressed by demons in their dreams. There is also one who is possessed and she is delivered as well. It does not take us long. We then go into classes, Marion and Mailes with the women and I with the men. It is dark when we quit. By the time we have supper, it is too late for anything else. All are tired and we turn in after some discussions. Marion and I are sleeping on the floor in a hut where I have been sleeping on previous occasions. No cockroaches, but there are noisy crickets. It's another dark night without a moon.

Marion and Mailes have heard from the women that the district chairman has a second woman whom he is seeing secretly. She is thought to be pregnant by him. He has been spending money on her that was meant for visiting churches. That is why so few are present for this seminar. After breakfast this morning, we hold a district meeting to elect a new committee. The old chairman is replaced with a new one. After the meeting we have a communion service. Marion and Mailes pass out the used clothing before we can leave for our next seminar.

It is two o'clock when we arrive at Mpulungu in Mbala District. People are already waiting at the church that is just outside of town. They feed us before we go into the service. About 650 people are present. Quite a few choirs sing before my message. Among those seeking help are three people who are possessed with traditional and ancestral spirits. One demon keeps reminding us it will not leave, that it has inhabited the woman for years. But we persist. Finally, half an hour later, the demon exclaims, "You are too tough!" and "You are so angry with me!" Then, to our surprise it leaves immediately! All three people had several demons each. There are tough demons in this district.

Marion and Mailes teach the women while I hold a district meeting to form a new committee for Mpulungu District. It is now to be separate from Mbala District. After supper there is another service where about 1,000 gather inside a grass enclosure. I am very tired but preach when asked to do so. The Lord anoints the message and many accept Him as their Savior. One demon possessed woman who said she is only oppressed, is delivered of her three ancestral demons. One demon said that he is a witchdoctor. It is 11:30 P.M. before we can retire for the night.

We are sleeping on the floor in one of the rooms of the vice chairman's house. During the night, a rat disturbs my sleep. It makes a lot of noise in one corner of the grass roof above our heads. Mailes helps Marion pass out the used clothing in the morning to the pastors and the cooks. I give songbooks and literature to those who need them for the new district.

In the worship service, the Lord again anoints the message. It is a wonderful time in the Lord with many amens! Many come for prayer when the altar call is given. We conclude with the Lord's Supper. The members of the choirs do not all come for Communion. I encourage them to accept Christ and live for Him. It is now midday. We eat something quickly and then show Mailes Lake Tanganyika before leaving for Isoka District.

I take the short cut to Nakonde that runs along the Tanzania border. The road is rough and slow going. The 200 kilometers takes us three hours. At Nakonde we check for a sewing machine that is going to the women at Chinsali for winning first prize in the sewing contest for Northern Province. We cannot find one in the shops and there is no time to look across the border in Tuduma, Tanzania so we carry on to Isoka, as we are running late.

We are two hours late when we arrive at 5:30 P.M. The tent is set up right away, as it is getting dark. The district chairman here speaks Swahili just as the chairman in the last district did. We eat and then hold a service in front of his house. I preach to over 100 who have gathered. Many are prayed for before it is over. Finally, we turn in for a much-needed rest. Marion is feeling rough. She has a sore throat. It is cold tonight. I hear lions off in the distance between 2:30 A.M. and 3:30 A.M.! It is coming from the hills to our east. The Luangwa National Park lies in that direction.

In the morning, we take down our tent and then wash up for breakfast. The church stands near the tarmac road so we drive there for our service. I preach and then pray for those who come forward. After this we observe the Lord's Supper. Following this, the women walk back to the house where Marion and Mailes have a class with them. I remain to teach the men and also to hold a district meeting. At noon we return to the house and Marion distributes used clothing to the needy and the pastors. Mailes assists her. After something to eat, we leave for Chinsali District.

The people are waiting when we reach our church in the town of Chinsali. We enter inside and begin the service right away. I have learned to be ready to preach at a minute's notice! The building is packed and many come for prayer after the message. We deal with four who are oppressed by demons and then one who is possessed. It takes at least an hour to drive them all out as they keep talking, talking, and not listening. I had to get tough, the most ever, to get them to leave! One of the demons said he comes from a witchdoctor. Tonight Marion and Mailes hold a service with the women and youth while I have a district meeting with the pastors and deacons. It is late so I turn into our tent without taking a bath.

We sleep quite well. Up at six as always and then take down the tent before breakfast that Marion puts together as no one has prepared anything. Marion and Mailes meet with the women for an hour before the worship service. After the message, the whole front and aisle is full of people seeking the Lord. I suppose many have come in preparation for the Lord's Supper that will follow!

When done, we wish to leave but food is ready so we stay to eat. It is noon when we start out for Mpika District. Finally we come across a sewing machine in one of the shops at Mpika. We buy one for the women of Chinsali that the District Chairman will take back to them for winning the sewing contest.

We carry on to the church at Mufumbushi Village where we usually hold our service in Mpika District. We go right into the service and again pray for those who want help after my message. There are three women who need deliverance. With the first two, the demons leave quite quickly but the third one takes us some time as they chatter too much. Besides ancestral and traditional spirits (Mulenga, Mwila, and Mwenya), there is one that speaks in tongues, another one lisps badly, and also the demon Kilimanjaro. Praise the Lord, she is finally delivered completely!

Afterwards we set up the tent and then it is time to eat. There is another service tonight where there are a lot of choirs and specials. I have a sore throat from dealing with the many demons recently, so it is Mailes who preaches. She does well and there are those who want prayer. It is windy and the tent is flapping about as we retire for the night. It will be cool tonight.

Up early, fold up our tent, and then go to eat which again is in a small room at the pastor's hut. In the district meeting that follows, a new district chairman is elected. Marion and Mailes have a meeting with the women as they are having problems among themselves. Marion gives out the used clothing afterwards. In the worship service we pray for the district committee before I bring the Word. Many want prayer. We close with the Lord's Supper. It all ends well. We say our farewells before leaving the church. Then we hop into the Nissan and leave for Lusaka. The trip goes well and we arrive home before dark. Thank you, Lord! During our ten days on the road, we clocked 3,000 kilometers.

All of us are tired. After we eat, we have a bath and

drop into our beds. Mailes is staying with us and will leave for her place in Petauke District the day after tomorrow. She and Marion still have work to do tomorrow, to prepare for the women's convention next weekend. We have to keep right on moving for things to get done, as it does not get done on its own!

Marion has had quite a few seminars and conventions for women on the district and national level throughout the years. She will bunk in with them and stay on campus during the whole time, leaving only when it is done. She loves teaching and preaching. Mailes has been her companion on most occasions, translating for her when necessary and also sharing the pulpit, as she too loves to teach and preach. Mailes has a terrific testimony of someone saved from the old life of tribal traditions to a life of following Christ with her whole heart. She and Oscar her husband are raising their family on Christian principles. Marion and I are thankful for the help they have been to us and to the church here in Zambia. Our prayer is that God will continue to use them.

Sixteen
Famine in Zambezi Valley

Marion and I arrive at the village of Jordan, east of Chirundu in Siavonga District, mid-forenoon. The site for our service is not far from the Zambezi River. About 300 are attending the meeting under this large shady tree. After some songs, I pray for twenty-five children who have been brought by their mothers for dedication to the Lord. After this I bring the message and many seeking salvation come to kneel in front. We also pray for the sick. Then we look after those who need deliverance and cast out the demons from seven of them who are possessed. Also, evil spirits oppress two other women. We bind those in the name of Jesus and command them not to harass the women again.

We watch the women cooking *nsima* in a large drum over an open fire. Marion takes her turn for a while at stirring the heavy gruel with a large wooden spoon. When done, some of that *nsima* is part of our meal along with goat meat and greens. Marion passes out all the used clothing we brought along before giving out maize to the needy. It is measured out into their containers from the fifty sacks that were brought in earlier. Many have brought only material for the maize to be tied into. After we are finished, children scramble for the kernels that have fallen to the ground. Not a kernel is left for the birds or chickens!

There is famine all along the Zambezi Valley. So we make another trip to Siavonga District. As before, we turn off at Chirundu and travel east until we reach the village of Jordan. Tembo the Regional Evangelist is already here. He came earlier with the lorry (truck) carrying seventy bags of maize from Lusaka. There are around four hundred villagers gathered for the service. Several Christians from Chiawa District have come today. Churches have already been planted in that new district east of the Kafue River, which flows into the Zambezi a short distance from here.

After a few songs, I deliver my message and many respond. Special prayer is offered up for the sick, plus for the three who are oppressed by evil spirits. There are also nine possessed with several demons each. One woman has eight of them. Most of them are traditional with some ancestral spirits. There is a snake and a religious one as well named Maria. This one takes the longest and I have to get tough with the demon before it gives up and leaves. It takes an hour to drive them all from the woman!

Two women have to be brought back as each one still has a demon in them that had remained hidden from us! They are driven out this time around. One of the demons that had just been cast out enters another person who is waiting to be delivered! The demon informs us about it when we start dealing with the possessed person. Then, before I can finish casting out all the demons from a yet another woman, a second demon-possessed woman comes hopping on her knees up to where I am! So now I have two of them, one in each hand. With pure determination on my part, the demons are defeated and driven from both of the women.

Marion and Tembo are helping me. We deal with a woman who has a demon that roars like a lion. Another woman has a demon that writhes around on the floor like a snake. I am unable to keep the person from twisting round and round. This demon is strong! One other woman has a demon that rolls her eyes backwards until only the whites are showing! There is also a demon that bends the woman so far backwards that she would have fallen had we not held onto her. It is hot in here and I am wringing wet when it is all over. Struggling with demons is strenuous work to say the least. It involves the physical part of man as well as the spiritual. I thank God for His renewing power!

The demons in this area are known to be powerful and many in numbers. These women have acquired them from certain dances they perform at the *ngoma* (drinking parties). The maize we have brought is distributed after the service.

*   *   *

Marion and I are up early and we prepare for my trip to Eastern Province. We load the used clothing into the vehicle and onto the roof rack. Eat breakfast and at seven I say goodbye to Marion and pull out of the yard. Fill up with fuel before leaving Lusaka. Run into some rain along the way but otherwise I make good time. I reach Njemi Village in Petauke District at noon. There is some disorder due to the rain that just passed through. While waiting for food to be served, I talk to Mailes, Chisanga, and Moyo about a rumor concerning Moyo's lifestyle. Hopefully, by the time I finish this trip we will know the truth.

Before the service, I also talk to Oscar and Mailes about moving to Lusaka with their children to assist the work at headquarters. I preach in the worship service that is held outside under a grass shelter. Many come forward for prayer. We also deal with three demon-possessed people. We successfully drive them out. They were traditional spirits that chattered in languages no one understood, just a jibber-jabber with lots of whooping.

I have the men during our hour of teaching, Mailes the women, and Oscar the youth. Moyo looked after the TEE tests as several pastors wrote their exams. After the classes, Mailes and I passed out the used clothing, women's material, and literature. The district meeting that started after supper lasted until 10 P.M. It is raining tonight. The leaders and I are sleeping in a vacant building that has been built for the schoolteacher.

It rained heavily during the night and even this morning. Two orphans received their allotments for this quarter. We finally start the service when the rain lets up. I preach on the Lord's Supper, and am blessed as we observe it. It is past 10 A.M. when we get done. Time to start for Mambwe District, so I load up Oscar, Mailes, and Moyo and pull away from Njemi Village amid goodbyes and songs by the choir.

Fill up with fuel when we reach Katete filling station. I take the bush road that leads to Mambwe District. We run into rain. There has been rain here as the low places in the road are filled with water. The Nissan manages to pass through all of them, including a soft section where a tractor is stuck. I pass around it in four-wheel drive. We travel 105 kilometers on this bush track before we reach our destination. Because of the rain, it is decided to move several kilometers further on to the school at Mfuwe, as there is no good shelter here for the proposed seminar.

When we get seated in the classroom, we are told to move, as we are too close to the regional airport. Soldiers are camped nearby to prevent any suspected disturbances from the former president Dr. Kenneth Kaunda. His wife comes from this area. So we all move to another building where we finally hold our service. As usual I preach, and then pray for those who need help. There is also one oppressed by demons and five who are possessed with them. All of them are driven out; one of them is a foul demon. Its stench hits me in the face when it leaves!

After the service, there is still a district meeting where the District Chairman is replaced. There are sixteen churches now in this district. Finally, we eat at 9 P.M. The last time we tasted food was in the morning before we left Njemi Village! I am spending the night in an empty building. The Ndaos are sleeping in the next room. When at last I lie down, it is 11 P.M.

The sun greets me this morning when I step outside. It has not rained here since our arrival yesterday. We actually could have stayed at the place where they originally planned the seminar. We were taken from place to place for nothing and losing precious time for teaching because of it. I have a nice shower in a grass enclosure. Fortunately, Marion put a small towel in the lunch basket as I forgot my towel for bathing. It's not big but it will have to do. I also forgot the folding chair I usually take on safaris. These chairs in the villages are getting to be too hard, having to sit on them for most of the day.

Breakfast is late this morning, so Mailes has her class with the women while Oscar has one with the youth and the men. Moyo gives the leaders their TEE tests and I fill in a couple of application forms for orphans. This is the first for Mambwe District. At 9:30 A.M., we finally eat. Then it is time for the service. The building is full, about 300 people. Before I preach my sermon, we pray for the new district committee and the women's executive that were chosen this morning. After the message, we pray then for the many who want help before observing Holy Communion.

There are two who are possessed and want deliverance. I dismiss the congregation before dealing with them. The demons are driven out rather quickly, especially from the second person. I can't believe it! The three demons came out within two minutes. Thank you, Lord, for the power that is in your name! Soon after closing the service, we leave for Chipata District.

An hour later we reach Chiparamba Village where our seminar is to be. Because of the heavy rains yesterday, very few have showed up. We are served food and then we go into classes with those who are present. Mailes again has the women, Oscar the men and youth, while Moyo takes care of the TEE tests with the pastors. I discover the orphan who has been sponsored by Kinderhilfswerk died recently of roundworms. How sad!

Many come in after dark, too late for a service. I inform them to be ready early in the morning. After supper, I turn in. We are sleeping in the district council building. It is kind of the officials for allowing us to use the rooms in their building, not only for sleeping but for eating our meals as well. It is a warm night and I keep waking up every two to three hours.

It is a humid morning, a sure sign of rain. The cooks bring us breakfast at eight. An hour later we go into our service. By now Mailes has given out the used clothing to the needy and the box of material for the women. An old woman, who I am told is mentally deranged, keeps coming inside the building where we are holding our service. She is following us around, it seems. (We saw her yesterday at the shop.) When they fail to keep her outside, I go over and bind the evil spirit in her. She quits struggling and falls to the floor. "Do I continue, or do I carry on with the service?" I choose the latter, thinking I may have time afterwards to further deal with her.

I preach the message the Lord has laid on my heart, and then pray for those who come forward. Before we conclude the service, the Lord's Supper is observed. We are unable to deal again with the deranged woman, as it is time to leave for our next seminar in Chama District, a distance of almost five hours from here. I feel bad about it, but many more need me at the next place. Just the same, "Why do I have to have such a tight schedule?"

When we reach Chankhalamu Village near Kasera in Chama District, we find about 500 people waiting for us under a mango tree. The service starts immediately and after some beautiful singing, I deliver the message. There is prayer for those who come forward, one of them for demon-oppression. Also, two demon-possessed persons are present. One of them has two dancing demons. It does not take long and they are driven out. Both people have been set free. Praise the Lord!

We eat finally at 4:30 P.M. Then, Mailes has a class with the women and Oscar with the men. Moyo again takes care of the tests for the pastors in the TEE program. Food is served again at 7:30 P.M., but I do not take any. I am still full from the last meal only three hours ago. There is a district committee meeting tonight that lasts until 10:30 P.M. I discover some of the churches are using the large drums and allowing the youth to dance! I soon discourage that. We are sleeping in the headman's house. I am using the same room I had on my last visit. The first mosquito of the night shows up, and I think I got it.

I sleep quite well, the best thus far on this trip. There is plenty of fresh air due to the windows being wide open all night. There is chicken and rice for breakfast. It's the same menu for each meal, and always so salty! Mailes meets with the women and they choose a new executive as the present chairlady has three demons and cannot read. Oscar talks to the leaders about a proposed clinic while I meet with the orphans and give the guardians their quarterly assistance from Kinderhilfswerk. I also take new applications. Before the service, Mailes hands out the used clothing and material to the women.

Before I can get into my message, a woman goes into epileptic fits. They bring her to the front and I pray for her healing. The Lord heals her! She is normal right through the service and even afterwards. There are others who come up for healing after my sermon, plus a woman possessed with three demons. They talk in the plural tense, using "we" a lot. It appears there is one that is the leader, as we hear one say, "Father, we will not go until you come too." One demon speaks in English and yet when we ask the woman after all the demons are out whether she knows the language, she replies she doesn't!

Holy Communion is served and many take part. The attendance is over 700. I receive several gifts afterwards, including rice and a chicken. We are fed yet at noon before we take leave for Lundazi District. An hour later we arrive at Chalilo Village where our convention will be held. We do not go into a service right away, as many have not yet arrived. This is certainly not the norm for me! While waiting Mailes and Oscar teach their classes, Moyo has the pastors write their TEE tests, and I deal with the orphan program. I also give the wheelchair we brought along to the disabled woman. She is overwhelmed with joy when she receives it! She begins showing off immediately, wheeling it around the compound.

Before the message, I take time to remove at least thirty charms from around the necks of children and women, plus around the stomachs of infants. The most I have had to do in a single service! The Lord anoints His Word and many come forward for prayer, including the sick. After the service, there is a district meeting where we discuss the church roof that I had purchased iron sheets for. It is crooked, and because they built walls wider than originally planned, the sheets are not enough. So now they will have to take it apart and redo it.

I turn in at 10 P.M. and sleep in the same hut I did last year. At midnight, the youth singing and the children screaming and running about awaken me. It takes some time before I can get back to sleep again. At 5:30, I am awake so I get up. It is 8:30 before we get our breakfast of tea and buns. Unbelievable how long it took the women to make this simple meal!

We observe the Lord's Supper before my message in the worship service. But before I preach, I again remove many charms from children and women. One girl has six of them around her neck! This district has really backslidden. After the sermon, we pray for those who come forward. There are many sick that need special prayer, including one who is oppressed by demons. We also cast out the two demons from someone who was possessed by them. When the service is over, I am presented with four chickens and the Ndaos receive two of them. They bring us a basket to put them into, including the one I got from Chama District. I tie it onto the roof rack.

We bid them farewell and leave for Katete District. The convention is being held at the Mponda Church this time. Many are waiting for us when we arrive. We have our service and after some songs, I preach and many respond. Then Mailes and Oscar hold their classes. We visit until food finally arrives at 8 P.M. No district meeting here in this district so we all turn in at ten o'clock. I am sleeping in a house where Oscar and Moyo are occupying the next room. Mailes must be with the women somewhere else.

I sleep quite well, and get up at 5:30 as usual. We do not eat until eight though. While we are waiting, Mailes has her women's meeting and I give out the orphan assistance to their guardians. There are two disabled persons here that need wheelchairs. In the worship service I conduct the Lord's Supper and pray for the new women's executive committee, before Oscar delivers the message. When the service is over we are given gifts of food and chickens. I now have eight of them and the Ndaos four!

Before leaving for Nyimba District, I fill up the Nissan in the town of Katete. At three o'clock, we reach the place of our next convention near the town of Nyimba. When we start unloading our stuff, we discover that four of our chickens are dead! They apparently suffocated because of being overcrowded in the basket under a hot sun. Got the women to butcher one of the survivors for our supper as the District Chairman thought we are first coming tomorrow! He had told the people that the convention would be on the 31st. He did not know that November has only thirty days! So what there will be for a service tonight is anyone's guess.

It rains in the evening. They serve us food before dark. People start drifting in slowly and by eight o'clock we are able to start the service. There are five choirs and after they render all their songs, I get a chance to share the Word. As I conclude praying for those who have come forward, demons begin manifesting themselves in a choir member. Before we can get done casting them out, a second choir member begins screeching. Some of the demons speak to us. They have traditional and ancestral names. I had to get tough with them in order to drive them all out! I did not count on dealing with demon-possession tonight, as it is difficult seeing their faces in the darkness. But we are successful in casting every one out of the two women. I end up all wet with perspiration.

The service we just held was on the long veranda in

front of this large building that once was a shop but now is empty because its owner passed away. The two who were delivered from demons sat right in front of me and could not escape the Holy Spirit's presence! I am told there was another woman who sat further back in the audience that showed signs of demon-possession. I did not spot her because of the darkness. The trouble light I had hooked up to the Nissan battery did not reach that far. We are sleeping in this building tonight. There are enough rooms to accommodate us.

We pack up this morning after breakfast and cross the road to the church. Mailes teaches the women while Oscar takes the men and the youth before service time. She also passes out the used clothing and the women's material. In the service we present the sewing machine (we brought along from Katete) to the women for winning first prize in the regional competition held three months ago. They had sewn the best child's dress. I preach and many of those who come forward after my sermon are young men. We also pray for one who is demon-oppressed and a woman who has demons that need casting out. This we do and she is set free.

I am given a gift at the end of the service. Then we are given food to eat before departing for Lusaka. Another chicken has died so that leaves me only four to be taken back for Marion. We make good time and reach home by six o'clock. Marion fared well during my absence. I am told that one of the passengers killed in the hijacked Ethiopian Airliner that crashed into the Indian Ocean off the coast of Seychelles several days ago was Mohamed Amin, the famous photographer. We have several of his books.

A group from Western Canada builds a staff house.

The Zambian and Ohio groups start the left wing of a hostel.

The Missouri group builds the hostel's right wing.

A group from Alaska works at the tabernacle.

Gerald Marvel teaching church leaders—Lusaka

Tim preaching, Reinhard and Marion—Livingstone

The Kelleys and the Kruegers help with various projects.

Marion speaks at the opening of the Mufuli Clinic.

An oversized homemade guitar

Onlookers stand by as I put up my tent.

A place to shower in the village

An outdoor latrine in the village

Construction on a plot at Livingstone

Hairdressers—Sarah, Brenda, Mailesi, and Monica

Bore hole with pump, near temporary church, Mukuni

We receive a goat as a gift from a church in Livingstone.

Ngoni warriors during the solar eclipse

Makishi dancer in north-western Zambia

Sylvester and Ndalamei hoist me high on my 68th birthday.

Colleen bungee jumps from Zambezi River bridge.

We go microlighting over Victoria Falls.

Tiffany and Natasha are baptized in the Indian Ocean.

Tim makes the jump successfully as well.

Colleen, Tiffany, and I go horseback riding.

The Uganda Choir and I tour churches in Germany.

Tiffany, Ellen, Gerald, Colleen, and Tim—Kampala

Mailes and the Zambia church welcome Mark and Amy.

Our clan comes together before our departure.

Mailes translates for Marion in services.

Leaders from Uganda, Tanzania, and Southern Africa

Colleen cuts the ribbon at the opening of the tabernacle.

A plaque honors our contributions to the Avondale plot.

Ebenezer Tabernacle at Avondale in Lusaka

We are honored at our farewell and given the name *Njobvu*.

Handing over flags to Don Riley at our farewell

We pose with our children—Kirk, Colleen, and Mark.

For our anniversary we go riding elephants.

I will miss the wildlife of Africa!

I pass the mantle on to Colleen.

The time has come to leave our beloved Africa.

Seventeen
We Move to Livingstone

We have just completed our six months of home assignment in the States and Canada, and are now back in Zambia for our last term as career missionaries to Africa. Our Nissan Patrol starts up quite all right. The Pajero that Murrays sold us before returning back to America after spending just four months in Zambia has to be pushed for a while before it starts running. Oscar and Mailes Ndao with Afunika Tembo and Chapamba Moyo have come to welcome us back on behalf of the national church. Sarah and Agnes, our two house girls, prepare a meal for us that is very tasty. I have missed their African cooking! I drive the national leaders back to their homes here in Lusaka. We turn in at 9:30 P.M. A cold bath tonight, as the hot water pipe is blocked!

Marion, Sarah, and Agnes have to clean the whole house. There are gecko droppings and dust everywhere. While in town shopping, I lock the door and forget the keys in the ignition. The spare set is not in my pocket so what to do? Of course, the young chaps watching the vehicles on the parking lot, crowd around now and show me keys they carry in their pockets. They do not work. One of them says they are for Toyotas. Someone comes up with a piece of wire and slips it behind the window. His endeavor to hook the knob inside fails. Then he tries to slide the wire along the outside of the glass thinking to hook the mechanism of the door handle. This does not work either. Finally, he reaches underneath the latch on the outside of the door and up pops the knob. I never knew that this could be done! A person keeps learning something new from the thieves here in Lusaka.

We are going to spend our Christmas and New Year's Day with the Stevensons in Uganda. A taxi is taking us to the airport. The driver has to add some fuel at Munali Filling Station before he even goes a kilometer. Most taxis I have ridden in Africa operate this way. They never fill the tank just add enough to get you to the next station! When asked why they drive like this, they answer me that they don't have the money to purchase more. The vehicle is smoking a lot. By the time we arrive at the airport, Marion has sore eyes from the fumes. I breathe in very little air along the way and so survive the trip.

The flight goes well. Tim and Logan are there to pick us up at Entebbe. It is after 10 P.M. before we arrive at their house in Kampala. Colleen and the rest of the children are still awake and waiting for us. It is 2 A.M. before Marion and I turn in. Not much night left anymore! And it is a short night because Tiffany and Natasha show up in our bedroom at 7:30 A.M. It is a custom they developed years ago. Another custom that they have is to ask me for a bedtime story before they go to sleep. How I manage to keep coming up with new ones is a miracle. Some are real accounts of my past, but most are invented at the time I am telling them! Reading a story from a book will not do.

Before the gifts are given out on Christmas Eve, the children have a song and we share some of our outstanding Christmases of the past. Then the gifts are passed out. The children are all excited by now! We are having a nice time with Colleen, Tim, and their children. It is great that our daughter cares so about her Mom and Dad. Tiffany is someone special as well. She is very inventive and has made for her mom a book with some nice sayings in it. There is plenty to eat and it is late to bed. And so another Christmas has come and gone.

To remember the end of 1997, we travel west to Mburo National Park and spend it camping where wild animals still roam. There is plenty of game; in fact, a herd of impala hang about camp most of the time. We sit around the campfire New Year's Eve and spin yarns until midnight. We wish each other a happy New Year! The Lord has been good to all of us, keeping us together as He has.

Two weeks with the Stevensons have passed so quickly and now it is time to return to Zambia. The whole family escorts us to the airport at Entebbe. We check in our luggage and then say our goodbyes. It has always been hard to bid farewell to Colleen and it is no different today. I cannot hold back my tears, and neither can she. We wave to them until we pass out of sight into the waiting lounge. The return flight is uneventful and we are back in our home before dark.

Five days later, January 8th, 1998, we begin our move from Lusaka to live in the town of Livingstone near Victoria Falls. A house has been purchased there for us. We want to start weaning ourselves away from the national headquarters in Lusaka. They must learn to handle more the administration of the church in Zambia, as we will be retiring in four years' time. The multi-purpose building built here last year contains office space for the national leaders. It was a joyous celebration the day it was dedicated on May 5th, 1997. We had representatives from Tanzania, Kenya, Uganda, Zimbabwe, Mozambique, and Malawi in attendance, plus the Minister of Religious Affairs for Zambia and Gary Kellsey from Western Canada. Our move to Livingstone will also help us plant churches in Southern Province.

We arrive in Livingstone just after one o'clock, making the 485 kilometers in five hours. We pick up the keys to the house from the previous owner, Wayne Wright, and then eat our lunch that Marion brought along. There is quite a bit of work to be done in the house before it can be liveable. The kitchen cupboards need to be replaced and a carpet put on the ironwood floor that is too warped to leave as is. A Dutchman from South Africa built this house back in 1949 with the customary two gables on the front side. The tax in that year was one cob of corn! Imagine?

We spread our safari mattress on the kitchen floor; it will be our bed tonight. The sleeping bag we brought along will not be needed, as it is too hot and humid. We talk a lot, planning the alterations that need to be made in the house and so we do not get a full night of rest. It is already 80 degrees when we get up in the morning. The altitude here at the house is 3,020 feet while at Lusaka it is 4,060. We are again in the land of the baobab trees! They were so numerous around Kaiti Mission where we once lived in Tanzania. The mist from the thundering Victoria Falls ten kilometers away can be seen rising up into the sky from our front door!

The last of our furniture and household effects finally arrive in a twenty-foot container from Lusaka. We now have all our things here. Wally and Gladys Krueger have come from Canada to help us with the renovations. Wally is kept busy for the next two months. Then we all return to Lusaka to welcome a group flying in from Western Canada who is going to assist in the building of a staff house and to erect a wall around the five-acre lot at Avondale where our national headquarters is situated. Many that we know from a way back are in the group that have come. Much was accomplished during the three weeks that the twenty-four Canadians were here.

We soon have a congregation started here in Livingstone. The services are held in one of the schools. I am their preacher whenever I am not away visiting the work in Zimbabwe, Mozambique, or Malawi. Marion fills in during my absence. Before long we also have a church operating in the town of Choma. First, Christopher Chimbwali assists us in Southern Province and then it is Conrad. Churches begin springing up throughout the districts of Livingstone, Choma, and Kalomo. Marion and I are soon kept busy visiting them all. As in other provinces, we register orphans in the Kinderhilfswerk program and enrol pastors in the TEE program. The needy soon learn where we live and make their way to our gate for assistance. The Lord keeps filling our jar and we continue to help them.

Marion checks with the police about helping the prisoners in their jail. They grant her permission to take them food that Shoprite discards from their store. The prisoners soon get to know her and are happy to see her pull up with the food. They shout to her from behind barred windows, "Thank you, Church of God, for the food!" She is able to help with the release of two men who had crossed into Zambia illegally. They are escorted back to the borders of Angola and the Congo where they had come from. She says there are more foreign prisoners that ought to be released.

We drive out to Nsongwe Village for a service. It is about 10 kilometers south of the town of Livingstone. This is a very poor area; everywhere huts are leaning precariously ready to collapse. Grass huts have not changed through the years. The church here has just been started recently. There are thirty-four of us gathered in front of an old man's hut. Marion shares before we sing a duet in the Nyanja language. I deliver the message afterwards. Four young men accept Christ. We also pray for two women who are sick. After the service, I fill in two application forms for orphans.

Before returning home, we drive to Mukuni Village. We hope to plant a church here. Dr. David Livingstone met with the chief of this tribe years ago when on his way to cross the Zambezi River. Chief Mukuni offered Livingstone twelve warriors to accompanying him into the interior. I am told that only two of them returned. The remaining ten warriors were never heard from again. The tree they both stood under is still standing!

Three weeks later a church is started at Chief Mukuni's village. It is an honor to be at a place where Livingstone once stood and talked to the ancestors of those who are gathered here today! I preach to fifty-two people who have gathered. Quite a few adults step forward to receive salvation. Praise the Lord! I am jubilant at having planted a church here in Mukuni Village where the chief has his boma (headquarters).

Reinhard Berle and Tim Stevenson come to visit us at Livingstone. While here, they check about some projects on behalf of Kinderhilfswerk. On Sunday we attend the service at Maramba here in town. Over 100 people are present. There is some nice singing in the Tonga language. Tim brings the message. For an illustration in his sermon, he climbs onto the table, grabs the rafter and pulls himself up! He is comparing it to "holding onto your faith." The people will not easily forget him, or the message! I enroll some new orphans for the Kinderhilfswerk program while Reinhard talks to the one who already is receiving assistance.

In the afternoon, I take the two men out to Nsongwe Village to check on the orphans there. Enroute we come across a herd of elephants just outside of town. They cross the road in front of us. It is a common sight during the dry season to see them feeding alongside the road between town and the Zambezi River. Baboons and monkeys are plentiful during this time as well. There are numerous species of wild life, including buffalo, rhino, and elephant in nearby Mosi oa Tunya National Park. Hippos and crocodiles residing in the Zambezi River take their share of humans who dare to paddle their boats haphazardly.

After taking photos of the orphans at Nsongwe Village, I drive on to Mukuni Village where Reinhard checks into the prospect of assisting orphans here as well. Joseph the church leader and I show him the site where we hope Kinderhilfswerk will put in a borehole so the villagers can have sufficient water. Joseph is one of Chief Mukuni's messengers. It is a good visit and we return home. It is late before we get to bed.

Two days later, we return to Mukuni Village to meet the chief. Joseph escorts us to his palace. We are told to kneel at the entrance, clapping our hands at the same time, before entering the palace. Then again when he actually comes over to shake our hands. There is a leopard skin on the wall and a lion skin on the floor in front of his throne. He is friendly and we visit for half an hour. The conversation also includes projects that we can help his people with. His chiefdom covers quite a large area. We come away satisfied with the visit.

On another visit, the Stevensons join us in a worship service at Avondale. There are 123 people present. Colleen and Marion sing a duet before Tim delivers the message. It is a good sermon. During the altar call, I have to call up two of the workers by name, as they are not coming up to repent. (They had been caught earlier in sin.) Others quickly rush to the front; afraid I may call their names next! They literally scramble over the benches and chairs. The Holy Spirit moves in the audience and the front is full of seekers. It is nearly a three-hour-long service.

Marion preaches in another service at Avondale, with Mailes translating. Many respond and come for prayer including a young woman possessed with many different demons. There is a lion, several ancestral spirits, a dumb one, and one who keeps saying, "No! No! No!" when I command it to come out. I have to wake her up a couple of times before she is finally delivered. It takes at least half an hour for them all to leave. I have been told that demons that say, "No! No!" or "Naught! Naught!" are religious demons. Also, those that say, "Yes! Yes! Yes!" Religious demons will also ask for a white cloth before agreeing to leave.

As in other provinces, we also come across many in Southern Province who are demon-possessed. Here are a few instances. At a service in Kalomo District, it takes me only five minutes to drive out the three demons that possess the woman. One is a snake that twists her around, another does a lot of screaming, and the third one is very passive maybe because it now finds itself alone.

While in a service at Kabuyu in Livingstone Province, Marion deals with two demon-possessed women. Conrad is assisting her. One has three demons and the second woman only one. Both women are successfully delivered. Another service at Kabuyu finds me present and this time three more need deliverance. One has nine demons, the second one three, and the last one is a man who was once a preacher but now is involved in witchcraft. The demons are all driven out from the three people.

At the church here in Livingstone, one Lozi woman is possessed with a demon that inhabits her legs, numbing them! The woman says that the demon has one leg, one arm, and one eye. It is the first one of this kind that I have come against. It is the demon's duty to now drive the person to a witchdoctor for help. Instead she has come to church. I cast the demon out of the woman in the name of Jesus!

After a worship service at Kanyama, we deal with a woman who has seven demons. One says to me in Swahili, *"Natoka baharini."* ("I come from the lake.") It must be from Lake Tanganyika. Another demon dances for us around and around! They all are driven from the woman and she is free of them.

We deal with a demon-possessed woman at Avondale who has twenty-two demons! Surprisingly it takes us only fifteen minutes to drive them all out. There were mostly lions, monkeys, and snakes. At one time she said they were all gone but kept on jerking the upper part of her body. I keep binding the demons as they were lying to us. I could see in her eyes there still were demons inside. Finally, they all are out. She is now herself and there is happiness on her face. Praise the Lord!

During another service at Avondale, there is again a woman possessed with twenty-two demons! It is her first time to church. It takes us about twenty minutes to set her free. There were: snakes, monkeys, ancestral, Judas, Satan, and a lying spirit that said they were all out but were not. The one called Satan reappeared after he had been cast out! Finally, they are all out. While driving out the demons, we were shown by the woman as to how many were still inside by the number of fingers she was showing on her hand.

A lady from Makeni who needs deliverance is brought to our house. It takes an hour for Marion and me to drive out the seven demons. The dumb and mad demons were very stubborn while the three ancestral spirits, snake, and lion demons came out quite easily. We had our hands full hanging onto her whenever the demons got violent. When she is finally free of them, she looks around bewildered. After figuring out where she was, she shakes our hands. The ordeal has left her exhausted.

She shares with Marion that she received the demons while she was still an infant. When her grandmother was dying, they took her and the infant to the river. There the baby was immersed in the water and held there for an hour until all the demons were transferred from the dying grandmother into the infant! The demons kept the baby from drowning, Marion is told. This woman, who has just been delivered from seven demons, is that infant! Hard to believe, isn't it?

Accounts of human sacrifices still filter through to us. It is an age-old custom that does not want to disappear completely. Innocent victims are sought for ritual ceremonies. It does not only take place in remote areas up country but in cities as well. I will not elaborate on this subject but give you one incident that took place recently near Avondale. A thirteen-year-old girl goes missing and a week later her sister finds her in tall grass near their garden. She has been mutilated. Her breasts, vagina, and internal organs have been removed. It was a ritual killing. This is by no means an isolated case. Sadly, similar accounts are reported much too often.

*   *   *

During our last term, all our travels to churches in Zambia were in Southern Province. Our regional evangelists are now traveling in their respective provinces doing the work that I used to do. Oscar, the national treasurer, and Moyo, the national legal representative, do a lot of traveling as well—including distributing orphan funds on my behalf. But Marion and I do squeeze in a trip to North-Western Province.

When we reach Mufuli Village in Kabompo District, we find many people waiting beside the road. They sing and ululate as they escort us to the site chosen for our meetings. Tembo, Oscar, and Kakinga the new regional leader, are present. The health post here that has just been completed will be officially opened tomorrow. CIDA (Canadian International Development Agency) and Sahakarini in Canada donated the funds for it.

We unload the medicines Marion brought along into the clinic. It is to be used by the male nurse for treating patients. When we wash up, we have to use a *chitenge* (piece of material) to dry ourselves with as Marion forgot the towel. So it's not only me, she too forgets to bring one along! We are served supper before the service. Marion shares and then Oscar preaches. It ends at 9:30, except for the singing that goes on into the night. We are sleeping in one of the rooms at the house built for the male nurse. The sponge mattress on the cement floor is our bed and our blanket is the sleeping bag.

We are up early and then it is breakfast time. The village headman brings us a rooster and some mealie meal. Marion passes them on to the cooks to make for dinner. Tembo buys some wild meat that is from a duiker. The choirs sing and sing until finally the district officials show up two hours late! Dignitaries from the health department, district administration, political party, and security have all come to the official opening of this clinic. We serve them soft drinks and muffins. After this there are speeches. Marion, who was in charge of this project, explains the purpose of this health post and what it has cost. The district administrator cuts the ribbon. The headman and Oscar give the closing remarks.

We eat dinner with all the guests. I have some duiker meat and liver. It is mid afternoon when all have finally gone. Tembo preaches tonight at the service. The local musical group here has homemade instruments; one of them resembles a guitar and sounds quite nice. It is 10 P.M. when we turn in.

I wake up with a case of dysentery. It appears the rest have it as well. It must be from the meat we ate yesterday. The service this morning is held in an enclosure where the people have to sit under the hot sun. There is a bit of a shelter over our heads. The Lord anoints the message and pretty well all come forward for prayer. We receive several gifts at the end of the service. After eating the food prepared for us, we leave for Zambezi District.

As soon as we reach the church we enter into a service. The building is full as it was at Mufuli. Again the Lord anoints the message and many respond. Orphans from Zambezi, Chavuma, and Kabompo Districts are present, so I give them their allowances. Some Angolans have come, including their district leader. The meeting with the pastors and district leaders takes until 8 P.M. to finish. We leave and book in at the Zambezi Motel for the night. The window in our room has broken panes, so I stuff the pillow into the openings to keep out the mosquitoes.

The mosquitoes get into our room anyway in spite of my endeavor to keep them out with the pillow. We can't use the blankets, as it is much too hot. So the mosquitoes have a feast! Up before six and an hour later we leave for Lusaka. All goes well and we reach the comforts of home before dark.

I have always enjoyed traveling to remote villages in the outlying areas of Zambia to hold services. I miss meeting those who have become my very close friends over the years. Each time I went I saw how they had grown spiritually from my previous visit. It is sad that these opportunities are not available any longer due to the expanse of the territory I now cover. My passion for African souls has so enlarged my tent that it is nigh impossible to visit them as often as I used to. Is this the price one pays for having too large a vision for the lost?

Eighteen
Highs and Lows

Another year, and another century has just ended! What will the year 2000 hold for us? There were times in the past year that brought us joy and tears. What will the new year of a new century, plus a new millennium bring? Mark, Kirk and his family are here with us. There is nothing much going on here in Livingstone to show that this is a special day! Hope Colleen is having a memorable time with her family in Uganda. I call her to wish them a Happy New Year. It takes a while to finally get through to her. They are still up. Tiffany comes on line as well.

The previous year we had spent a wonderful Christmas with the Stevensons in Kampala, Uganda. Tim's parents, Gerald and Ellen from Malawi, were present as well. Marion and I had actually gone there not only to be with family for Christmas but also to take part in their TEE graduation ceremonies. At that time I handed out several certificates. It was an honor to give Moses Abasoola his diploma for finally completing the third course. He will be representing Uganda at the upcoming World Conference to take place in Britain.

I need to mention that Moses accompanied the 1995 Uganda Choir when they toured the churches in Germany. I happened to be on a speaking tour at about the same time and shared in some of their services. During my three weeks in Germany, I preached in most of their churches without an interpreter. My German got better the more I used it. Definitely a high point for me! Also, got to speak at one church across the border in Holland. I stayed with Reinhard and Irmgard Berle when not on the road. He had me travel from town to town by electric train. A great experience!

We invite Ignatius to visit Zambia. He is one of the church leaders in Uganda and is married to Mary whom I ordained a few years ago. Both of them were some of our first converts when we went to Uganda back in 1983. I have written about Ignatius suffering persecution for the Lord's sake in my book *Amid Perils Often,* chapter seven. Oscar Ndao escorts Ignatius to some of the churches in Lusaka and in the districts where he shares his testimony and the Word of God.

At our executive committee meeting, Mailes shares of her trip to Uganda where she had been invited to be the speaker at their Women's Convention. She speaks very highly of Tim and Colleen Stevenson, and how the church is so mature in Uganda. She challenges the Zambian leaders to push ahead. The final reports show that the total number of churches presently in Zambia, January 2000 is 646 with 77,500 members! This is the highest yet thus far. In our Sunday service, I preach on "Turning the World Upside Down for Christ!" The Lord anoints the message!

During the executive council meeting, both Mailes and Marion are ordained in a Sunday service at Avondale on April 9, 2000. Gerald and Reena Marvel from Vancouver, Washington are present to assist in the officiating of this monumental event! This is the first time that women are being ordained in the Zambian Church of God. It is only my second time to ordain an African woman; the first one being in Uganda a few years ago. Gerald brings the message afterwards and many come forward for prayer. It has been a very good service!

The Marvels have come to assist us with the Leadership Training program. There are forty-three leaders present for the weeklong classes. I happen to have my sixty-eighth birthday at this time. When I arrive from town where I had gone for some supplies, Oscar calls me aside in order to tell me something. I am suddenly grabbed by some of the leaders and placed onto an armchair. I am then lifted up above their heads and they begin carrying me into the hostel. I bob up and down as they march along, robustly singing songs of praise. At the dining room, they stop and two offer up prayer for their beloved missionary. What an honor! The whole incident is quite moving! This is one birthday I will long remember.

We attend the meeting in Lusaka when Jane Goodall arrives to give a lecture on chimpanzees. It is special for us to hear her speak. Twenty years earlier, when we were still missionaries in Tanzania, we had dropped in at her research station at Gombe, Tanzania, on the shores of Lake Tanganyika, and seen the chimpanzees for ourselves. I make mention of this in *To a Land He Showed Us,* on page 200. She has written several books on the chimps she has studied.

As an author of several books, I am especially excited about meeting another author. He is Norman Carr, the author of several wildlife books. Once a game ranger, he is the first person to introduce tourist safaris to Northern Rhodesia, which today is Zambia, and pioneered walking safaris. Carr is the founder of the Wildlife Society of Zambia. The list goes on and on of his accomplishments. He is eighty-four years of age when I meet him at Camp Kapani along the Luangwa River where he lives. We talk for half an hour and then I return to my writings for the next book.

Tiffany Stevenson is not only interested in hearing my stories, but is able to tell some of her own. In fact she has been jotting down short stories in notebooks since she was very young. She penned one in 1995 when she was just nine years of age entitled "The Adventures of Anna and Hanna." She is quite an artist as well and the book contains some of her drawings. I found it interesting enough to have it published in Lusaka for her twelfth birthday in 1998. I would like to think that I had something to do with her talent for writing. Whenever I was around her, she made sure I told her several stories before she dropped off to sleep. Therefore, it is no surprise to see her writing short stories of her own.

The following amusing incident bears repeating. Thieves break into a house at Kanyama by hacking their way through the back wall. They find the occupants sleeping on just a mat. There is nothing else in the house. The thieves are upset and ask the couple where they are from. The man answers, "From Mbala." So the leader of the gang gives them a blanket and enough fare money to go back to Mbala. Then he tells them, "We don't want to see you here tomorrow. If we do, we will kill you. You have wasted our time and energy, so be off!"

The General Assembly revises its *Constitution and Bylaws* in September 2000 and certain changes are made as far as titles are concerned. The Legal Representative is henceforth to be called the National Church Representative. The National Chairman is now National Overseer; the Regional Evangelist is now Regional Overseer, and the District Chairman is now District Overseer. Three months later, another first takes place when Reverend Mailes Ndao is appointed to be the National Church Representative of Zambia. The first woman to be in this post! She is a very special lady and rightly deserves this position.

The second wing of the hostel finally gets done and we have the opening on December 3, 2000. All the church leaders have come in to celebrate this grand occasion. John Campbell and Harry Ukrainetz are our special guests from Western Canada. I offer up the dedication prayer and John cuts the ribbon. We now have ample room to accommodate all our national and regional leaders plus missionaries. The structure includes an office, waiting room, kitchen, dining room, laundry, and bathrooms.

Annually for the past three years, we have had groups come out from our Living Link Churches in the States on work camps to help us in our building program. In May 1999, a group came out for two weeks from Springfield, Ohio, and worked on the hostel building. Pastor Brent Farmer, and longtime friends George Reed, Larry and Wanda Ditty are part of the group. An event took place that everyone will long remember. Sylvester, one of our leaders, came down with cerebral malaria. Early one morning he begins to wail, claiming to have had four visions. They are about wars, a funeral, and Christ's soon coming. He quickly becomes a nuisance around the place. He reminded me of William Madebe when we worked in Tanzania. He acted like this when he came down with cerebral malaria. (*To a Land He Showed Us,* page 213.)

Sylvester goes around telling some of the leaders, including one American, that they need to repent! At one point he gets all the leaders to go and see the missionary. They come to the office and stand in front of me waiting for what I had to say. Of course, I know nothing about this. He had fooled them all! Quite a joke, but it wasn't meant to be one. After a few days, Sylvester is back to his old self. He is a fine young man, a faithful servant of the Lord.

In June 2000, a group flew in from Rolla, Missouri, to assist us further with the hostel building and to also erect a second staff house. Pastor Pat O'Brien and his congregation have been a longtime supporting church. Then, a group comes from Anchorage, Alaska in August 2001 to work on the big tabernacle. They also have come for two weeks. Their pastor is Brad Sutter. Others in the team are Ralph and Ellie Sutter, Hui Le, Bob Hopkins, and Jill Kaniut, to name but a few. Jill's father, Larry Kaniut, is an author and has written several books on bear tales and survival stories in Alaska. Looking forward to meeting him when on home assignment.

We have the work groups that come out from the States and Canada participate in weekend services. The first one is usually at headquarters and the second one at a village church. There they will observe their joy in the Lord as they worship Him in spite of living in terrible poverty. Of course, they will also witness those who are possessed by demons and need deliverance. As well there is time set aside for a safari into a game park to view wild animals in their natural habitat. Victoria Falls is always a must to see and then a sunset cruise on the Zambezi River.

It is always a huge loss to the church when top national leaders pass away, resign, or backslide. I have been in Africa long enough to have witnessed the fall of several leaders from the pedestal we helped to put them there. The biggest disappointment is when a man in high position is proven guilty of a sin he has committed, but refuses to repent, and then retaliates.

He first tries to take the church to court for dismissing him from his post after finding him guilty of immorality. When that fails, he attacks the missionary accusing him of character assassination among other things. The very things he is guilty of himself! I had to appear in court several times, and my wife once. The end result is that he fails to wrangle a large sum of money from me and to deport me. The judge finally orders the lawyers to settle out of court, stating that this is a church matter. When the two of us meet, I go the second mile by shaking his hand and telling him to let bygones be bygones. The case is dropped.

I want to add that the National Executive stood with me throughout this whole ordeal that lasted for more than two years! The Lord also faithfully stood by me, His servant, who had all manner of evil said against him falsely. The portion of Scripture recorded in Matthew 5:10–12 became very real to me during this whole period. I had never before been so attacked by anyone as I had been by this fallen church leader. What has happened to him? He is back to where we first found him. The Word clearly states, "Pride goes before destruction, and a haughty spirit before a fall." (Proverbs 16:18)

It is rather interesting that when dealing with demons they can pass on information in unexpected ways! For instance, while casting out demons at a service in Kanyama, one says to the national leader who is assisting us, "You are making too much noise! My ears are closed. You are annoying me. In what way are you going to chase me? You are my friend!" Then, in another service at the same place, one demon says to a different national leader, "I will not go, I know you. You are one of us!" Were they right? The two leaders left the ministry soon after.

The Lord has at times made me aware of upcoming

events in dreams, preparing me for what lay ahead. I need to say this before I carry on any further. I am seasoned enough to know the difference between a normal dream and one where the Lord is trying to reveal something of importance to me. Acts 2:17 says: "Your young men will see visions, your old men will dream dreams." I have experienced both during my forty-four years in the ministry—thirty-seven as a missionary in Africa and seven as a pastor in Canada.

It usually pertains to national leaders whose names I will not mention. Here are a few of those warnings. The first one I wish to share is as follows. I am awakened from a dream in which I am on a stairway. I suddenly trip on the steps but catch myself in time on the railing and do not fall all the way to the bottom! Is it a revelation of what I just was going through with a certain leader? Must be as there were hands reaching out to help me that I would not fall down the steps.

In another dream, I am in the bush hunting and wound a hyena. It runs off and I try to track it down. Finally, I hear it making a noise. Then it comes running from a thicket right at me laughing hideously. I shoot at it and discover that I had not put a round into the barrel! Too late, it is upon me. The hyena then turns into a large black figure in front of me. It is Satan! I wake up. It is 3:30 A.M. To my mind comes the interpretation that one of the national leaders who has been wounded, is going to retaliate. And it will be at me! I have been forewarned in order to be prepared.

In a different dream I find a particular leader in a room on his knees. One of the other leaders there informs me that he is in deep trouble. Others are looking on. I wake up. Is the one on his knees in trouble? If so, it will be revealed. Or, do we pray that it will be avoided? Well, a few months later, I do discover that he is in financial trouble up to over his head! To escape a prison sentence, he ends up surrendering all his possessions in his house to the one whom he owed this large sum of money.

I dream one night where I come upon one of our leaders in a darkened room. He slips out when I look in on him. Acted like a thief who does not want to get caught! Does it mean that this leader did steal the checks that have gone missing from our post office box? Donations from abroad have not been turning up. It turns out that this is the man who has been stealing them!

Another time, I dream that a large vehicle like a bus looms abruptly in front of the one I am driving. Before we collide, I am startled awake! Does this mean that there is an impending confrontation with the national leader who has been trying to involve me in his case with the church? It appears inevitable? I am being drawn into a case whether I want to or not. Lord, help me. And thanks for the warning!

In another dream, I am beside a river erecting a miniature-sized church on its sandy bank. Then, one of our national leaders appears and begins to push the building toward the river where the sand starts to give way. I object to his plan and immediately wake up. Is that what he is up to, to wreck the church? He will not succeed as the church belongs to the builder who is Jesus Christ. I again have been forewarned about this leader's intentions.

Last night I dreamed I am up high repairing a water tank. It is frightening for me to be up so high. Then suddenly I have the job completed! It is hard to believe that it is done. Is the meaning of this dream that God will see me through this ordeal today? It is a day Marion and I must appear in court as witnesses for the police in the case over the checks that were stolen from our post office box. The Lord does stand with me in this case onto the end.

Besides these forewarnings, there are times when I am on the road driving or sitting at home, a foreboding of something about to happen grabs me in the pit of my stomach and my heart begins to pound. Am I being nudged to pray for someone in particular? I have learned that when this happens to quickly take the time and find out what it is, or for whom to pray! I bring before the Lord names of those who I think might need my prayers immediately. I usually start with my children. Is there one of them that is in some kind of danger or in a serious problem? When I discover the source, the foreboding subsides and leaves!

I have had other attempts to slow me down in my zeal and passion for souls in Africa. Accidents can be a common cause to accomplish this, and I have not been exempt from them. An example of one accident takes place in the Mozambican bush, which I have already recorded in chapter seven. I carried on with my journey in spite of suffering a severe whiplash from that fall. The after effects of that accident stayed with me for a couple of years, but never enough to keep me down.

The ceilings in our house are eleven feet high. Houses that Europeans built in earlier years had high ceilings so that the heat had somewhere to go since air conditioners were not yet a common item fifty years ago in many parts of Africa. So, the next best thing is to install ceiling fans. So, while standing on a ladder that is leaning against the wall in our spare bedroom, it slides along the floor and I crash with it on top of a metal chair beside the bed. It is a long fall and I end up bruising my shinbones, scraping my arms, banging my little finger, and splitting my left eyebrow. My glasses scratch the area around my eye as well.

I am fortunate not to lose the eye or break any of my bones! The metal chair has to be straightened as it got twisted from my fall. Did I do all that?

The Stevenson family, Marion and I drive out to Chindukwa Lodge, 28 kilometers west of Livingstone for the day. Colleen, Tiffany, and I go on a trail ride, as all three of us love horses. Our guide leads the way and soon we are in tight bush where we have to duck branches that nearly unseat us several times. We see monkeys and baboons. We also come close to a herd of elephants that are feeding in the heavily wooded area along the Zambezi River. Our horses spook but we manage to rein them in. We are riding single file and I choose to be in the rear so as to take pictures with my video camera.

As my horse comes up the dry creek bed, I come face to face with a large overhanging branch. I duck and am promptly squeezed against the saddle when the horse passes under it. My video camera is pinned under my rib cage. There is excruciating pain as I feel something give in the right side of my chest. I slide out of the saddle and double up with pain. I hear Colleen up ahead ask, "Are you all right?" I manage to gasp, "I am okay." I do not want to alarm her or spoil an otherwise nice day. I manage to crawl back into the saddle by standing on a fallen tree. The pain increases with each step the horse takes. I grit my teeth and make it back to the lodge. I now inform them of my accident. Tim drives us home.

The long and short of it is the X-ray shows that one rib is fractured and another one torn from its socket. It is loose and slips out of its socket whenever I get up from bed or a chair. My rib cage is taped so as to prevent this from happening, but it is more of a nuisance than help. The physiotherapist gives me several infrared treatments to speed up the healing process. It takes two weeks before I no longer hear or feel any grating noise when I move. The bruise on my shoulder where the branch hit me and scraped off some flesh is mending as well.

Tiffany and Natasha act as my nurses while I am recuperating, sometimes a little too rambunctiously! Regrettably, the day comes though when they must leave. The girls each leave nice notes for their Opa and Oma. In fact, we keep finding their notes everywhere in the house. This is a common occurrence ever after. They use the names Marion has given them soon after their birth—Princess for Tiffany and Kitten for Natasha.

You may wonder why I took the time to share a few of my accidents since everyone has one or more throughout their own lifetime. I did it so that you may know that I too am not exempt from physical attacks, and that they did not remove me from the battlefront. My passion for Africa is far too great to give up!

Nineteen
On Livingstone's Trail

It is only fitting that I make some mention of a man who has come to mean so much to me in Africa. He is someone who has already gone on to his reward more than 130 years ago. Yet, it is as if he still walks this land! I used to read about him before coming to this continent. And ever since my arrival, his life has become even more inspiring to me. Maybe because I have crisscrossed his paths often in my own wanderings across much of his and my beloved Africa! There are those who say that he did not convert many people. That may be so but what we need to remember is that he was a medical missionary. He has left a legacy behind in that field. Besides this he opened up his Africa to missions through his boundless energy in exploring the unknown regions. Who am I talking about? It is Dr. David Livingstone.

While still living in Tanzania, we as a family make a trip to Kigoma on the shores of Lake Tanganyika. It is in August 1974. On the way we stop for the night at Tabora, once known as Unyanyembe prior to the colonial era. Several miles outside of town we find the house where Livingstone and Stanley stayed for several weeks back in February and March 1872. When the two part company on March 14, it will be the last time that Stanley will ever see Livingstone alive. Henry Morton Stanley had been sent by the *New York Herald* newspaper to find Livingstone, who had been reportedly killed by savages in dark Africa. Many failed to accept this report and Stanley is given the task to find the now famous missionary and explorer dead or alive.

Marion, the children, and I travel on to Kigoma to visit the Marrows, missionaries with the Baptists. We also drive out to Ujiji just south of Kigoma, a small town on the shores of Lake Tanganyika. There is a large stone marker on the spot where Stanley finally found Dr. Livingstone standing in front of his hut on November 10, 1871, after having spent seven months traveling 800 miles from the Indian Ocean through hostile territory. It is a privilege to stand where they had stood! I can almost hear Stanley utter those now memorable words, "Dr. Livingstone, I presume."

The two became fast friends. It was a father-son relationship. Stanley, an orphan, now had found a father he so needed in his life. Livingstone influenced much of the young man's life during those four months they spent together. After he hears of Livingstone's death, Stanley returns to Africa and endeavors to continue the work of Livingstone in trying to find the source of the Nile. But as it turns out, he discovers the source of the Congo River and follows it all the way to the Atlantic Ocean. Because of many bouts with malaria, Stanley too dies early in life. He is only sixty-three when he passes away, not in Africa, but in Britain.

One of the white men accompanying Stanley on some of his future expeditions is William Hoffmann. He was with him in early 1887 when they crossed the interior of Africa from the west coast to the east coast. After leaving the Congo River, they crossed through western Uganda and northern Tanzania, all familiar territory to me.

Hoffmann went on to lead two expeditions of his own into the Congo, the first one in 1881. Is he my distant relative? My grandfather John Hoffman dropped the second "n" from his family name after migrating to Canada. I would like to think that William is there in my roots. How else can I explain this passion for Africa? He loved Africa as I do.

While in Kenya, we as a family fly over to Zanzibar and see for ourselves one of the world's most beautiful islands. It is known for its famous clove and cinnamon trees. We pass through the coconut plantations until we reach the slave caves and walk inside them. Here is where thousands were imprisoned waiting to be shipped to points east on Arab dhows. Near the harbor stands the house that Livingstone lived in while outfitting his last expedition in February/March 1866 for the mainland. Amazingly, today, April 1, 1975, it is still standing! Not far from here is the house of Tippu Tip, the notorious slave trader.

It is not until we move to Zambia before I again am back on the trail of David Livingstone. It is June 7,1994, when I first visit the city of Blantyre in Malawi. Beginning in 1861, Livingstone, along with other missionaries who heeded his call, labored here and as far north as Livingstonia on the western shore of Lake Malawi (previously known as Lake Nyasa). Many died of malaria but others survived the harsh surroundings they found themselves in. A church was soon erected at Blantyre during 1888–1891, which is still standing today. Beautifully colored windowpanes grace the walls inside. Livingstone himself named this place after his hometown in Blantyre, Scotland where he was born March 19, 1813. Today we have many churches scattered through this area.

Marion and I have stood on the shores of Lake Malawi several times and watched the sunrays sparkle and shimmer on the waters at sunrise. Livingstone walked this shore as well and sailed on this beautiful lake many years earlier. Boats carrying human cargo were transported across this lake on their way to the coast and then to the Arab slave markets. The sight so appalled Livingstone, that to his dying day, he fought to end slavery in Africa. A month after his death this evil curse was finally broken.

Livingstone used the Shire River to get from the Zambezi River to Lake Malawi. It was laborious work maneuvering their boat over and around the rapids that exist between the two points. I have traveled this section many times by road. On one safari, I take time to check on the whereabouts of Bishop Mackenzie's grave. It is buried in the swampland of Elephant Marsh on the southern end of Malawi. Oscar and Chomanika are with me. We turn off northeast at Bangula and travel down a gravelled road to what remains of Chiromo, a village that died when the Shire River flooded it and the lowland in 1979. A few broken foundations still remain where once buildings stood. Chomanika points out the school he taught in years ago. It is now beyond repair.

We enter a wooded area and commence searching for the grave of the Bishop who succumbed to malaria January 31, 1862, only a year after his arrival to Central Africa. Livingstone visited this site sometime after hearing of his death. The bush is very tight and the trees so entangled that we are unable to make much progress. Thorns snag our clothes at every move. We finally come across three graves of young men who died sometime after the bishop's death. It is sad that no one has been looking after these long forgotten graves now sorely overgrown with thorns and vines. We call off our search but will resume it in the morning. The locals are asked to clear a path for us into the heavy undergrowth.

As planned we show up the following day and find that the locals have chopped a path into the bush where there are more graves. The floodwaters of 1979 have destroyed some of the markers. We discover the resting place of Mackenzie surrounded by several other graves. His grave and the one beside him are in bad shape. He had laid down his life for the gospel's sake far from his native home, only to be forsaken in death on the foreign field!

The Shire River flows out of Lake Malombe, which in turn receives its waters from Lake Malawi. While in that vicinity in late December 1995, we traveled up to Monkey Bay and then on to Cape Maclear where the family and I did some sailing and snorkelling in the quiet waters of Lake Malawi. Livingstone traveled much in this area during his Nyasaland expedition from 1858 to 1863. His footsteps can almost be seen on the lakeshore if you look closely. Is it my imagination!

My first trip into Mozambique in order to start registering the church was to Tete the capitol city of Tete Province on June 8, 1994. It lies due south of the town Katete, Zambia. There still exists an old fort here on the Zambezi River that the Portuguese built and managed during the days of colonization. Livingstone made many stops here as he struggled to find a water route into the interior. Because of the Kebrabasa Rapids just west of Tete, his project failed. Today the Cabora Bassa Dam stands at that site. Tete is headquarters for our church in Mozambique. As the town was a stopover for Livingstone, so also has it been for me.

A feat no white man had accomplished previous to the time of Livingstone was to cross the continent of Africa from coast to coast. This he did by boat, oxen, and on foot. To reach the west coast, he started out from Linyanti in today's Botswana on November 11, 1853. He uses the Zambezi River to cross into Barotseland (western Zambia) passing Senanga and Mongu along the way. When he is beyond the Kabompo River, he enters Angola just east of Chavuma. He leaves the Zambezi River behind him and heads in a westerly direction overland until he reaches the west coast at Luanda on May 31, 1854. After he spends four months at Luanda, Livingstone retraces his steps to Linyanti on the Chobe River arriving September 10, 1855.

I shared in chapter twelve that I have been to Luanda on several occasions, the first one being January 14, 1999. The Atlantic Ocean that Livingstone looked at, I have looked at from that very town. The fort in the city was there at that time. When I visit the congregation we have at Viana several kilometers outside the city, the church leader said "It is a real honor to have the missionary here in our midst. It is like a dream!" The honor is mine, to be at a place where Livingstone had reached many years earlier. And now I have done it as well!

On November 3, 1855, Livingstone departs from Linyanti and sets out for the east coast. He spots on the horizon clouds of vapor rising heavenwards. Next he is gazing at a gigantic precipice with a churning and thundering body of water! He has reached Mosi oa Tunya, the Smoke that Thunders. He names the now famous Victoria Falls after Queen Victoria. On this historical day November 16, 1855, he exclaimed, "We look and look again, and hope that scenes lovely enough to arrest the gaze of angels may never vanish from memory."

Because of the many rapids to Kariba Ridge, Livingstone now takes an overland route that passes through

Kolomo and Monze until he reaches the Kafue River. Here he finds wild game abounding in large numbers. He follows the river to where it joins the Zambezi. Then it is on to Zumbo where the Luangwa River empties into the Zambezi. When he nears the Kebrabasa Rapids, he skirts around it on land. Before long he is back on the Zambezi and is carried downstream past Tete, Sena, Mutarara, Shupanga, and finally to the east coast arriving at Quelimane on May 20, 1856. He has completed his journey across the continent of Africa! A remarkable feat of endurance!

Except for the interior of Angola, and that is because of their civil war, we have planted numerous churches all along his route from the east coast to the west coast of Africa. Livingstone not only opened the way for the early missionaries but for us as well who have come more recently. His life influenced the beginning of many missions after his death. Africa would soon no longer be called the Dark Continent.

On one of my trips to visit the churches in Mozambique, I take the time to look for the site of Mary Livingstone's grave. She had passed away on April 27, 1862, at Shupanga Mission situated on the banks of the Zambezi River. Her husband David had done all he could but malaria fever claimed her life. It was a sad day for Livingstone to lose his wife who had returned from Scotland to be at his side after years of separation. He was a broken-hearted man.

On October 13, 1996, I am traveling north from Beira to the Zambezi River on that forsaken road that is fit only for 4x4 vehicles. Moyo and Chitui are with me. When I reach the road that turns off to Lacerdonia, I take it. It is practically an unused road. Trees have fallen across it and we have to detour around them. At Lacerdonia we find deserted buildings. It is a ghost town. People who used to live here have long fled because of the civil war. Several miles further along on what was once a road, we arrive at Shupanga Mission.

The sign at the entrance is still standing and so are many of the buildings on the station. But there is no one around! What was once a flourishing place where Livingstone and others lived and worked is now empty and lifeless. Graffiti covers the walls of what was once a beautiful church. The roof is missing, the iron sheets carried away by soldiers or rebels. The remains of what must have been the clinic where the good doctor once labored stands rundown and forlorn. We look for the graveyard and find it on the edge of the compound. Mary's large gravestone is easily spotted standing in the shade of a large tree. It is surrounded by several other graves. She is not the only one to have laid down her life.

Today we have many churches throughout this area. After we return to the main road near the small town of Caia, we cross the Zambezi River on a ferry that is large enough to carry several vehicles and passengers. The river is quite wide here. The Portuguese had wanted to build a bridge to span the river but never got around to completing this project because of the bitter civil war. The 200 kilometers to Quelimane is a nightmare. The tarmac is all broken up and the big bridges are blown out of commission. The last 20 kilometers are so full of holes that it takes forever to get to the city.

This is where Livingstone stayed from May to July 1856 and then in February 1858 he was appointed Her Majesty's Consul at Quelimane, much to the chagrin of the Portuguese. Besides the Arabs, the Portuguese were also involved with the transportation of slaves on the high seas. Livingstone returned in January/February

1864 during his travels along the east coast of Mozambique. Many years before this, in 1498, the Portuguese explorer Vasco de Gama landed here on this coast. To his surprise he found a black Muslim community of traders already in existence. This city has a long history. There is a Catholic cathedral in the middle of the city that was built around 1776.

While on a visit to South Africa, Marion and I drive out to Kuruman near the Botswana border. It is June 7, 2001. I want to see the place where Livingstone started his ministry under Robert Moffat who had built a mission station out here among the Bechuana tribe. At the town center is a large spring called Kuruman Eye. From it Moffat dug a furrow to bring water to his station five kilometers away. Livingstone arrived here from the Cape on July 31, 1841, a young man at twenty-eight years of age.

We visit the church that was built on the station where Moffat and Livingstone worshipped. We walk the garden paths that David Livingstone walked with Mary the daughter of Robert Moffat. There is still the bench where they sat and discussed their future. After a short courtship, they were wed on January 2, 1845. But before this takes place she nurses him through his injuries, which he suffered when mauled by a wounded lion February 16, 1844, leaving him with a permanently shortened left arm.

It is very informative and educational to be here where these men of God labored so faithfully out in wildest Africa. May I rise to the occasion to always do my utmost for Him! I am so thankful for the privilege of serving my Lord for the past forty-three years. One more year to go and we will be terminating our full time service in the ministry. It has been a marvellous journey thus far. Their passion for souls in Africa has been mine as well.

It is in Zambia that I find most of David Livingstone's tracks. I am crossing them almost everywhere we plant a church. When he traveled from Malawi to Lake Tanganyika on his last journey, he passed through Chipata, Katete, and then across the Luangwa River to Mpika, Kasama, Mbala, and finally Mpulungu on the shore of Lake Tanganyika. Then he trekked westwards toward Lake Mweru passing places such as Nsama, Kaputa, Mporokoso, Luwingu, Mansa and Samfya, (today's towns) to mention but a few. These are all places where we have been, preaching the Gospel at our churches in northern Zambia.

It is here in the swamps of Lake Bangweulu that Livingstone finally succumbs to malaria and dysentery. For a week he has been bleeding from his intestines. He dies while kneeling beside his bed in Chitambo Village the night of May 1, 1873. His days of trekking central Africa have come to an end. This great man finally ran out of health and endurance. Two of his faithful servants, Susi and Chuma, now remove his heart along with his internal organs and bury them under a tree. There in the soil of Africa, his heart mingled with the land he loved and gave his life for. Then they proceed to salt down his body and dry it in the sun. After that is accomplished, they commence the longest funeral march in history, carrying the body of David Livingstone 1,500 miles to the coast reaching Bagamoyo ten months later in February 1874.

Who says that he did not have any converts or a following? Who today would risk their lives to carry someone of another race all that distance through hostile tribes in order that their beloved friend could be buried among his kin? Only those who truly had the love that their friend had for them. "Greater love has no one than this, that one lay down his life for his friends" (John 15:13). Records show that many of Livingstone's servants and followers went on to become pastors and evangelists for the Lord.

I arrive at the Livingstone Memorial in Chief Chitambo's village on August 20, 1995. It is a dream fulfilled for me to finally reach the spot where he died on his knees while praying. The hut is gone and so is the tree, but the spots are well marked. It is a memorable experience for me to stand at this hallowed spot where this all took place so long ago, but not to be forgotten.

At Bagamoyo, Livingstone's body is placed aboard a ship and Jacob Wainwright, a follower of Livingstone who speaks English, accompanies it to Britain. He is buried with honors in Westminster Abbey, London, on April 18, 1874—the only pauper among royalty. On his tomb they inscribe these words: "For thirty years his life was spent in an unwearied effort to evangelise the native races, to explore the undiscovered secrets, to abolish the desolating slave trade." And then his last words, "who will help to heal this open sore of the world."

Marion and I drop in to see his grave on one of our flights through London. We walk through the Abbey and see where the greats are buried including David Livingstone. I get permission to take a few photos of his burial spot. The guide has the crowd move back so that I can take the picture. He introduces me as a missionary coming from Africa where Livingstone had traveled and died. Before leaving, Marion and I sit on one of the benches and have prayer. I have to weep as I remember what the Lord was able to do through Livingstone in Dark Africa. I am challenged to carry on my quest to take the gospel as far as I can.

Zambia has done well to keep the memory of Livingstone alive. Even the town Livingstone, where we eventually live for four years near Victoria Falls, still bears his name. A statue of the man stands at the rim on the Zimbabwe side of the falls. I have crossed over twice to Livingstone Island situated at the edge of the falls in the middle of the Zambezi River. Mind you it can only be done during the dry season when the river is quite low and rocks are sticking up out of the water. It is here that Livingstone dared to measure the depth of the falls by using his primitive tools. Yet his measurements proved to be amazingly accurate!

Not far from the town of Livingstone is Mukuni Village. I have already mentioned earlier that it is here that David Livingstone meets with the chief. His footprints are everywhere throughout this area. What an honor to have lived where he walked!

Twenty
Out of Africa

As time draws closer to our departure from Zambia, and Africa, we try to do all the things that still need to be done. There are two things though that are not going to take place and that is to plant churches in Namibia and Botswana. Missionaries are not coming to assist me and I have reached the end of my physical limits. On a trip Marion and I made to Windhoek, Namibia, in September 1998, I had checked with the authorities about starting churches there and was given the go-ahead. As for Botswana, we have had contacts there across the border for years. Recently we took the Stevensons there for an outing. It would have been great to include the two countries into our sphere of work in Southern Africa.

Missionary Retreats in Africa are held annually, usually in Uganda, Tanzania, or Kenya. But in April 1999, we host it at Livingstone. Besides viewing Victoria Falls and a sunset cruise on the Zambezi River, there are quite a few other attractions in this area, two of them being micro lighting and bunji jumping. Surprisingly, ten missionaries take the jump from the bridge that spans the Zambezi River between Zambia and Zimbabwe, Colleen and Tim being two of them! I had been looking forward to doing it as well but my busted ribs kept me from making the jump. As for ultralighting, we have taken this scenic flight over the falls.

The following Missionary Retreat is at Siana Springs near the Masai Mara National Park, Kenya. Then, in April 2001 it is at Mombasa on the Kenyan coast. Jim and Dulci Doty from Angola are present. There is a farewell party for Marion and me where we receive many accolades from the missionaries. An album was put together and presented to us. It contains photos of us and of the work we did, plus many letters. It is a memorable occasion! Sunday is Easter Sunday so the Stevenson family, Marion and I get up early to hold a baptismal service at sunrise. Tiffany and Natasha want their Opa to baptize them in the Indian Ocean, which I do. It is a special occasion for us as a family!

Tiffany is now attending Rift Valley Academy just where her parents went when they were her age. While having Christmas with the Stevensons in December 2000 and watching Tiffany pack her bags reminded me so much of the times I would see Colleen doing the same thing years earlier, sitting cross-legged on her bed deciding what things to take and what not to take with her. It was always an emotional time for us as it is now for them as a family. Gerald and Ellen Stevensons, plus Mark and Courtney are present this Christmas in Kampala.

Through the years we have seen several lunar eclipses. The last one is on January 9, 2001, while we are in Lusaka. The moon began to disappear at around 9 P.M. and an hour and a half later it had disappeared completely. Total sonar eclipses are not as common but we have witnessed a few of them, the last one being on June 21, 2001. It happens to be a very special eclipse as it corresponds historically with another total eclipse that took place back in 1835. The Ngoni tribe in South Africa began migrating northwards after the death of Shaka Zulu. There is a total eclipse of the sun the day they cross the Zambezi River and invade the Senga tribe in Zambia. They go on to conquer many more tribes all the way into Tanzania before they run out of steam.

Oscar, Mailes, Mailesi Phiri, Sarah, and Monica are with me as we travel to Luangwa where the historical crossing took place back in 1835. Marion is back in Livingstone and will watch the eclipse from there. Visitors have come from all over the world to Zambia to view the solar eclipse. Along the way we stop to take some pictures at the unnamed hot springs 85 kilometers east of Lusaka beside the Great East Road. It is quite a phenomenon, yet unnoticed and untouched thus far by tourism.

The ceremony commences with traditional dancing and a speech from the chief. This takes place as the moon begins to make its way across the face of the sun. Warriors take to their boats and re-enact the crossing of the river to Zumbo and then back again. There is a mock battle where the Ngoni defeat the Senga. The total eclipse takes place at 3:15 P.M. It cools off drastically and it does get quite dark! Among the photographers present is CNN (Cable News Network). We leave at 4 P.M. but do not get back to Lusaka until midnight. The vehicle heats up and then stops near the springs. We try pushing to get nearer to the water, but finally give up and flag down a vehicle that tows us to Lusaka. It has been quite a day, and night!

What a thrill it was to have finally taken a ride on an African elephant! Marion did it as well. It was on our anniversary. We accomplished this across the border in Zimbabwe. The Stevensons did it a year later. I will miss the African bush with all its wildlife, and the walks Marion and I would take to look at the seventh wonder of the world, namely, Victoria Falls. What a sight! One day when the Stevensons are with us, we stop at the hotel near the falls and find Arnold Schwarzenegger and his family enjoying the scenery as well. No need to add that he is a huge darling with the city dwellers in Zambia who have access to TV and videos.

Marion and Colleen fly to Kentucky for our son Mark's wedding that takes place October 20, 2001. He had met Amy Perry in Lusaka where she had come to assist the Baptist Church with their youth program. They are now involved with youth and projects in our church in Zambia. Hopefully, they will be able to fit into the work so soon after their wedding.

We undertake to build a tabernacle at Avondale the final year we are on the field. It is to seat 1,000 people. We begin in January 2001 and manage to complete it by December. There are setbacks along the way but with His help we make it. The tabernacle is dedicated December 15, 2001. We have invited representatives from Malawi, Mozambique, Zimbabwe, Uganda, Tanzania, and Kenya to this big event. Around 500 are present. The Stevensons are here and so are the Rileys. Tim and Mark are able to install the sound system in time for the service. Marion has composed a song, "All the Glory Belongs to Him," which she sings backed by the choir after my message and before the dedication prayer. A very fitting song! The words and tune came to her from the Lord one night a couple of weeks earlier.

The following day is our farewell. Kirk surprises us and shows up in the morning from Harare, Zimbabwe, where he is still employed by UNICEF. We now have our three children together for this special day! There are at least 600 present for the service that starts at 10 A.M. Lots of special singing, choir numbers, and speeches from country representatives before the message from Don

Riley. Then Marion and I give our farewell remarks. During this time, I hand over the flags of Malawi, Mozambique, Zimbabwe, and Angola to the Regional Director for Africa. Chomanika, Chitui, and Guni are now under his administration.

Next, I hand over to Mailes one of my walking sticks and pass on my authority to her to lead the people of Zambia. She nearly collapses from surprise and sobs brokenly on my shoulder. Finally, I place the mantle I had specially made for Colleen around her and charge her to continue serving Him faithfully. I do the same with the mantle for Mark. It is the first time that I have performed this kind of a ceremony. I used the illustration of Aaron and his rod for Mailes, and Elisha receiving a double portion from Elijah for Colleen and Mark. God blessed mightily this exercise in the program. It spoke volumes to the African.

Before the end of the service, we call up Kirk and lay hands on him and pray a blessing over him. Marion gives him the quilt that she made for him. On it is a scene of Mt. Kilimanjaro and elephants. Marion spent months working on it. Colleen and Mark have already received theirs sometime back.

Guni, Chitui, and Chomanika hand me their reports for the last time. There are 250 churches in Zimbabwe with 18,350 members. Mozambique has 294 churches with 45,328 members and Malawi has 188 churches with 32,193 members. Joao Antonio did not come from Angola where there are eighteen churches and 1,930 members. I leave with one regret that I was not able to plant churches in the interior of Angola as I did in the other countries. Their civil war prevented me. Zambia's latest report is that there are now 522 churches (down from the last report) with 62,441 members. I am disappointed; the regional and district leaders are not performing their duties. Must missionaries still be out there?

In the afternoon we gather again in the tabernacle. Marion and I are escorted from the hostel to the tabernacle amid singing and dancing by the women. Flowers are tossed on us as we march along. Inside the tabernacle a red piece of cloth has been placed in the aisle for us to walk on to the platform where we are then seated under an arch. The front is beautifully decorated with roses, two zebra skins and one from a leopard. In all 1,000 roses have been bought from a nearby estate for our celebrations! We are given many gifts plus more accolades. There are speeches and songs. We are treated much like royalty! They give us African names. Mine is Mandala Njobvu and Marion's is Taonga Njobvu. *Njobvu* is elephant in Nyanja.

We have packed the things we are taking to Canada and the shipping agent is able to stick all the boxes into three crates. In a couple of days they will be on their way to Calgary, Alberta, by air. All our children and grandchildren, except for Courtney and Sean, are here for our last family Christmas in Africa. We take time to spend a couple of days at Lilayi Lodge where we relax and watch some wildlife. It is nice to be in the bush again! It is a memorable occasion, one that Marion and I will always remember.

The three men—Kirk, Mark, and Tim—run out to Kafue Flats to hunt for lechwe. By night they have not returned. We are in bed when they finally pull in after midnight all muddy including the two vehicles. They had trouble getting one of the vehicles out of the mud where it had gotten stuck in the middle of the flats. They still managed to each shoot a Kafue lechwe. It is not often that Tim has a chance to go on a hunt and so he thoroughly enjoyed this one mud and all.

On the last day of 2001, Oscar and Mailes Ndao invite Colleen, Tim, Marion, and me over for tea, *chitambua* (similar to doughnuts), and groundnuts. It is a nice visit. We will miss their fellowship after we leave in a couple of days. They have been steadfast in their walk with the Lord and in their service for Him. Then, we as a family stay up until midnight to usher in the New Year. Marion reads Scripture and has prayer. We are in His hands for another year. How different it will be for us to be far away from family and Africa.

The grating call of a francolin awakens me to my last morning in Africa. The radio warns people to stay home due to possibilities of rioting in town over election results last week. Most shops are therefore closed. At three o'clock, we all leave for the airport. The lorry is going as well, loaded down with those who want to see us off. After we check our luggage through, we spend the last few moments with family and our Zambian friends. The choir sings for us right here inside the airport. I pray for them, we embrace, and amid tears we say our goodbyes. It is always hard to say goodbye to Colleen and even more so this time. We both weep, realizing that no longer will we be working together in Africa.

Our family and the Zambians wave to us as we board the plane. Once inside my tears run unashamedly when the plane taxis down the runway. As it lifts off into the sky, the jet has all to do to break the tie that has bound me to this continent. Our career has finally come to an end. No longer am I their missionary.

Africa is setting me free and allowing me to leave her soil that at times in the past it appeared she might claim me for her own. But, alas, she has had compassion on me and I will be buried in my native land. Not that I would have minded being drawn into her bosom when taking my last breath. I will long cherish the times spent with you, beloved Africa.

It is not easy to write gracefully without a certain amount of satisfaction about the part we played in pioneering and evangelizing the work in Africa. During those thirty seven years Marion and I labored in ten countries, most of those as pioneers. In total, we were instrumental in planting 2,260 churches and leading at least 214,500 souls to Christ! Most of those results took place during the latter half of the thirty-seven years. Without our leadership and dedication they would not be there. I say this to honor and glorify our Master who made it all possible. The Lord looked for someone and He found Marion and me to do the job! And we did it.

The Parable of the Talents (Matthew 24:14–30) has an interesting lesson in it that many fail to see. Everyone has been given at least one talent according to this parable. But not everyone uses it for the master. Therefore, it is taken away and given to the one who has been using all of his. The one with the ten talents receives it, not the one with five. Why not even things out a bit and give the one talent to him who had five? Because he who had ten had already proven that he was more capable of handling twice as many talents. He was the better choice out of the two to be trusted with another talent!

When Marion and I went to Africa back in 1959, we probably had one talent each. But because we were eager to do all we could for the Master, talents were added to the ones we had. Marion, who did not know about delivering babies, suddenly was able to do it! We who had never taught in Bible School now taught and trained pastors. (I did not come to the mission field with any degrees. They came later on in my ministry, and after retirement.) We were not taught how to cast out demons, yet God gave us that gift. Country after country was opened and when no one came He endued me with extra strength and power to fill in the gaps left by those who did not come to assist me. We even stay on the field five years longer than required!

If I look again at that Parable of the Talents, I have to come to the conclusion that there were those with a talent each whom the Master had given to be used in Africa. Because they did not heed the call to go to the mission field lost their talents to us so that the work could get done, plus the blessings that could have been theirs came to us instead! Matthew 24:28 states: "Take the talent from him and give it to the one who has ten talents."

*   *   *

We are on home assignment for the next six months traveling to our supporting churches in the States. The ones in Canada will have to wait until we terminate with Outreach Ministries the first of July and have moved to our new home in Alberta. One of the first things we do is purchase a vehicle. This time it is a Ford Explorer and not a Nissan Patrol. It serves us well as we travel from state to state sharing what God has done in Africa. We meet Mike and Karen Isaac who will be going to Zambia in early 2002.

We are pleasantly surprised when Mailes Ndao, Colleen, and Natasha fly in from Africa in time to attend the ceremonies at Warner Pacific College on May 4, 2002, when Marion and I receive our Doctorates of Humane Letters. They stay on for the International Convention held annually in June at Anderson, Indiana. So for a month all three travel with us and help speak in the churches. What a blessed time we have together!

The church in Uganda ordained Colleen in March 2002. How proud we are of her! There is nothing too difficult for her to do. She not only travels in Uganda but to Rwanda and to troubled spots in the Congo as well for the Lord. She could write a book or two of the adventures she has had. Tim and Colleen have also reached out into Burundi, Sudan, and Ethiopia. They are a couple who are eager to serve the Lord to their fullest!

Tim, Tiffany, Jesse, and Logan fly in the week before the convention. We all carry a flag for the Wednesday night missionary service. The Stevenson family are again commissioned to the mission field. Marion and I feel very much left out this time! There is a farewell reception for us at Park Place Church after the service. Many of the older missionaries are present. Doris Dale is in charge of the program. Colleen and Tim speak and so do we. Global Missions present us with a plaque and a gift. It hits me once more that we are not going back to the field! We still are having withdrawal pains.

We meet Jim Nipp, whom we have not seen since he and his wife left Tanganyika (Tanzania) back in 1963 for Bechuanaland (Botswana) where they successfully started a work. They make their home now near Anderson, Indiana. Word comes to us from Colleen that Rufus Akhonya, who assisted me in Kenya and then in Uganda, has gone on to be with the Lord in August 2002. He was a faithful servant and remained steadfast to the end.

Colleen and Tim also inform us that the volcano near Goima in the Congo has erupted and hot lava has spilled into town. The roads to Sake and Gisenyi have been destroyed. There is hot lava everywhere and still spewing from the volcano. Tim has been there and the residents will need assistance to rebuild their houses once the volcano quietens down. This volcano has been a menace to this area even long before I first visited this place back in 1984. Lava is strewn throughout the whole area giving evidence that there were many previous eruptions.

All too quickly it is time for Mailes to return to Zambia. The end of June we drop her off at the airport in Indianapolis on our way to Alberta. The Stevensons make their way up to Canada by road and help us get settled into our new home at Black Diamond, Alberta, which lies just southwest of Calgary. We had chosen this place back in April when we made a trip to see where our future home will be. It was decided to sell our house at Carstairs and buy here at Black Diamond where there is a beautiful view of the Rocky Mountains. The house we choose butts against a large ranch with an alfalfa field right across the back fence. Deer, elk, coyotes, and plenty of gophers inhabit the area. No elephants though!

Even though we no longer are employed by Global Missions as of July 1, 2002, we keep visiting our supporting churches in Western Canada the rest of the year, slipping in and out of homes touching lives for a moment. In July the Stevensons and we are missionary speakers at the Western Canadian Camp Meeting. In a retirement service Marion and I are honored for our years in Africa as their missionaries. A week later the Stevensons leave us for Eastern Canada. Then they fly on to Uganda. It is the end of an era! Our daughter is leaving us behind in Canada and soon we will be continents apart. For seventeen years we were missionaries on the same continent but now it has come to an end. There is an ache in my heart as she drives off with her family.

We are to meet again briefly in April 2003 when Gardner College honors Marion and me with Doctorate of

Divinity degrees. This time Colleen brings along Tiffany when she flies in from Uganda to attend this special day in our lives. Courtney, who already is in Canada, attends the function as well. Work camps are planned for the summer of 2003 when Marion and I will again step on African soil, even if it is for just a few weeks.

Our house is beginning to look like home. African curios, pictures, and trophies clutter the walls upstairs and downstairs. Whenever I sit in my easy chair and look at all this around me, I am reminded of adventures on the African savannah. The drums in the corners stand silent. Yet they ushered us into Africa when we arrived, and they ushered us out when we left. I yearn to visit with those from that faraway continent, to hear again their voices.

Yes, I have plenty of snapshots and movies of our years in Africa and often I look at them. These possessions are mementos of when I moved with African friends, stalked wild game, and visited with family. Even as I write this book, my diaries will not let me forget those bygone days in Africa.